Tyranny's Al

Tyranny's Ally

America's Failure to Defeat Saddam Hussein

David Wurmser

The AEI Press

Publisher for the American Enterprise Institute
WASHINGTON, D.C.
1999

Library of Congress Cataloging-in-Publication Data

Wurmser, David.
    Tyranny's ally : America's failure to defeat Saddam Hussein / David
Wurmser.
        p. cm.
    Includes bibliographical references and index.
    ISBN 0-8447-4073-X   — ISBN 0-8447-4074-8 (pbk.

    1. United States—Foreign relations—Iraq. 2. Iraq—Foreign relations—
United States. 3. United States—Foreign relations—1989–1993. 4. United
States—Foreign relations—1993. 5. Arab countries—Foreign relations.
6. Hussein, Saddam, 1937– .
    I. Title.
    E183.8.I57W87 1999
    327.730567—dc21   98-31896
                                                                  CIP

1 3 5 7 9 10 8 6 4 2

The AEI Press
Publisher for the American Enterprise Institute
1150 17th Street, N.W., Washington, D.C. 20036

To my wife Meyrav—a source of inspiration, intellectual challenge, encouragement, humor, and happiness— without whom I would have neither the energy nor the patience to write

Contents

---------------------- ✦ ----------------------

Foreword

On November 12, 1997, David Wurmser published an article in the *Wall Street Journal* entitled "Iraq Needs a Revolution," wherein he emphasized that no strategy existed behind the U.S. policy on Iraq and that this failing would lead to a U.S. defeat. It was an understanding many others at the time had reached as well. Concerned by the dangerous deterioration of America's position on Iraq and in the region, the American Enterprise Institute convened a study group that resolved in its first meeting to urge the Clinton administration to pursue an *overt* strategy of insurgency. The Iraqi National Congress could lead such an insurgency. The study group accordingly drafted a letter to President Clinton calling for a policy shift and outlining the principles, tactics, and objectives of a plan to remove Saddam Hussein. With dozens of prominent and bipartisan signatories, the letter was privately delivered by Stephen Solarz and myself to National Security Council Adviser Sandy Berger in late January 1998.

It was our hope that the Clinton administration would view the receipt of this letter as an opportunity to extricate itself from the predicament into which it had wandered—a predicament that resulted, in large part, from the stubborn embrace of an oft-failed, moribund effort to oust Saddam Hussein *covertly*, through coup plots. That failed effort left the administration with only two options for reacting to Saddam's obstruction of UNSCOM inspections: to retreat, or to bomb Iraq. Of course, the United States had neither domestic nor international support for bombing Iraq, nor a clear plan as to how the action would contribute to Saddam's eventual defeat.

After the administration failed to embrace the suggestions outlined in the letter and began instead its process of retreat, the study group publicly released the letter, on February 20, 1998. This public release launched a (primarily) congressional effort to persuade the administration that current policy was leading to defeat and that an alternate strategy should be considered. Throughout 1998 Congress passed numerous bills demanding that the administration disburse funds to the democratic Iraqi opposition for an insurgency. But the Clinton administration repeatedly rejected, even ignored, congressional legislative efforts.

The United States faced yet another acute crisis in the autumn of 1998. With the administration still having taken no steps to craft a coherent strategy on Iraq and with the policy of retreat having resulted in a series of embarrassing events and high-level resignations, Saddam Hussein obstructed UNSCOM inspections once again. American policies lay tattered. Facing intense congressional pressure, the administration began to accept rhetorically, albeit grudgingly and evasively, elements of the insurgency strategy. The president signed the Iraq Liberation Act in September 1998 and reaffirmed his support for it in his speech to the nation in November, as he announced the cancellation of a series of airstrikes on Iraq. Still, the administration refused to commit itself unequivocally to a new strategy, raising questions as to whether any meaningful shift had occurred in U.S. policy.

This book provides a full explanation and detailed analysis of the assumptions and reasoning underlying the effort to change the administration's policy toward Iraq. It depicts the evolution of U.S. policy toward Iraq since the end of the Persian Gulf War and critically examines, sometimes without mercy, the basic elements and objectives of our current policy, persuasively arguing that it rests on defective foundations. The book explains in particular the danger, as well as the misplaced persistence, behind the administration's efforts to seek a coup at the unfortunate expense of a democratic insurgency.

But this book is about more than Iraq. It is an investigation that utilizes the Iraq issue as a magnifying glass to examine the thinking that has led to the persistent failure in the U.S. approach toward the Middle East. This failure stems from both the curious ideas about American leadership and the abysmal state of expertise that are held by many regional specialists, particularly in our intelligence community. It is unfortunately a failure to which many policy makers who are often *not* regional specialists are exposed.

The dire implications of this lack of expertise may be illustrated by my personal experience while working for Senator Henry Jackson in 1979. At that time the shah of Iran was teetering on his throne. Encamped with his spokesman in a Paris suburb was a shadowy figure known as the Ayatollah Khomeini. These men would appear routinely in front of their house and make statements widely carried by the news media about events in Iran. After some weeks, a distinguished scholar—I believe the preeminent scholar—of the region, Professor Bernard Lewis, telephoned me and said that if he heard another reference to "this mysterious figure Khomeini" he would scream. There was nothing mysterious about the Ayatollah Khomeini; he had written several books, and his activities were well known. Bernard could not fathom why everyone found it so difficult to understand the ayatollah. I asked him to tell me more, and he read me some passages from Khomeini's writings.

As a young Senate staffer, I knew I was hearing sensational material that had to get publicized in the United States. I suggested that Professor Lewis send me an Op-Ed piece that I could forward to a friend at the *New York Times*. He did so, and I duly passed it along. But a few days later my friend at the *Times* called to tell me that the newspaper had refused to run the piece; they had checked with the spokesman for Khomeini in Paris, who claimed it was a fabrication— that Khomeini had never written such a book, or any book.

Well, this seemed a slight hiccup, but surely not an insurmountable obstacle. When I asked what we could do, my friend suggested that we find someone to validate the existence and text of the book. At the time, I thought this would be an easy task. So I called the Senate liaison for the CIA—a very good fellow named Jack Murray—and asked for a favor: Could he ask the Iran analysts at the CIA to take a look at a photocopy of one of Khomeini's books and authenticate it? It had to be a photocopy; recognizing how transparent his purposes would be if the book were generally available, Khomeini's people had gone to great lengths to remove copies from library shelves all over the United States and Europe.

Jack came back a couple of days later and said we had a problem: nobody in the CIA was prepared to authenticate this book. In fact, nobody was convinced that it was not a forgery. I passed this reply back to Bernard Lewis, who was incredulous. Here was the team assembled to advise us about events in Iran, at a historical moment when a crucial decision, or sequence of decisions, had to be made about our policy toward the shah and his continued tenure, as well as general events taking place in Iran. Yet the whole bunch of them were so ignorant of the crucial underlying facts that they could not even speak to the authenticity of a photocopy of a book that had been in print for several years.

These shocking revelations illustrate the importance of David Wurmser's inquiry into our policy toward Iraq—and his broader effort to open a debate about the premises and quality of our Middle East policy makers and scholars. In fact, the relevance of this inquiry extends beyond our Middle East policy. During the cold war, in which I had a policy role, the United States focused primarily on the Soviet Union. We believed we would win or lose that war in Europe; fortunately, we won. But the spirit and lessons of that victorious effort were never systematically applied to regions that at the time were peripheral for the United States but have since become important. The principles on which the cold war victory was built only sporadically informed U.S. policy toward Latin America, and they affected our policy toward the Far East, Middle East, and Africa to an even lesser extent. In fact, many of the assumptions and ideas that led the United States into a dangerous position vis-à-vis the Soviet Union by 1979 survive to this day in our policy toward other regions.

Two of those assumptions in particular inform much of our policy in the Middle East. First, that policy holds that toleration of tyranny, rather than support for freedom, best secures stability, which is our supreme national objective. Second, many regional analysts believe that a strong, resolute, and unapologetic American defense of its interests would be regarded regionally as provocative and insensitive, and would therefore thwart our influence and foster anti-Americanism. Because of such views many of our regional specialists betray profound embarrassment, rather than faith and confidence, in the inherent correctness and appeal of our ideas. Thus they are attracted to policies that embrace local despots and establish our anticolonial credentials by displaying self-effacing, self-excoriating behavior.

It is hardly surprising that in the Middle East these ideas and the policies based on them have led the United States consistently into defeat. Our failure has disheartened those who wished to carry our standard in the region; it has emboldened, indeed confirmed, those who promoted hatred of America for political traction.

Tyranny's Ally challenges those flawed ideas. It will usefully guide policy makers in dealing not only with Iraq but with the Middle East as a whole. Moving well beyond today's headlines, it uncovers much about the assumptions and history behind currents of thought animating today's Arab politics. It is ultimately a broad-brush study of how the United States must deal with the sort of tyranny that consumed all of our attention during the cold war and continues to thrive in other parts of the world. This book should shake to its core the policy community whose failures, in the Middle East and elsewhere, erode and may begin to reverse that hard-won victory of the cold war. David Wurmser's proposals represent a solid first step in an effort to consolidate the victory earned in 1989–1991 in Europe by expanding it to other regions, rather than allowing our failures in those regions to haunt, and eventually endanger, our victory over communism.

RICHARD PERLE
Resident Fellow,
American Enterprise Institute;
Former Assistant Secretary of Defense
for International Security Policy

Preface

This book began as a report to be used as grist for discussion in a study group, first convened in the autumn of 1997, sponsored by the American Enterprise Institute. The concept was presented publicly in a *Wall Street Journal* article on November 12 of that year. At about the same time, Saddam Hussein initiated a series of crises that have been disturbing the international community ever since.

I decided to convert the study into a book with two objectives. First, I sought to provide a scholarly grounding for the effort surrounding the February 20 letter that urged the administration to consider the study group's proposed policy changes. Second, I recognized the need to clarify the context and assumptions behind the suggested changes.

To accomplish these objectives I first had to relate the history of our Iraq policy since the close of the Persian Gulf War. Chapters 1 and 2 focus on the repeated and unsuccessful covert efforts of the United States to launch a coup to remove Saddam Hussein. Chapters 3 and 4 address the question that recurs whenever I consider the history of Iraq policy: Why, if the coup policy is so obviously a failure, do we keep reverting to it? This question relates critically to the vision of our Middle East policy establishment; many of its decades-old core assumptions are simply flawed. To paraphrase Winston Churchill, the holders of these assumptions lack imagination regarding tyranny and evil. Chapters 3 and 4 examine the disparity between our Middle East policy and our deeply held contempt for despotism—the affliction that blights much, though not all, of the Middle East's politics. This deep and widespread political evil resists change despite its record of failure. The second half of the book moves away from the debate over first principles and back to the region's present political currents and strategic environment. Chapters 5 through 8 effectively outline a way for the United States to create a robust, integrated team around Jordan, Turkey, and Israel to secure our regional interests.

As I began writing this book I was startled to find, when giving presentations to informed audiences—typically, to groups concerned specifically with foreign affairs—that they were surprised by what I had to say. These audiences urged me to publish my information— particularly that regarding the floundering policies of the CIA. Yet, save for a few interviews with Warren Marik and Ahmad Chalabi, virtually all of the information in this book derives from the mainstream English-language media—the *Washington Post, New York Times,* and *ABC News.* A small portion comes from foreign press sources like the *MidEast Mirror,* widely available and read by regional specialists. None is derived from any classified or otherwise exclusive source.

In fact, rarely has a foreign policy issue been so thoroughly publicized. Decisions and policy debates even about covert actions have been aired for a remarkably prolonged time. Much of this information has surfaced because so many people within the decision-making community were disturbed by the direction of policy—most conspicuously, Scott Ritter, who resigned from UNSCOM and went to the press with his revelations. And the Clinton administration itself, determined to justify its policies publicly, has revealed a great deal.

The high-volume revelation of information on U.S. policy toward Iraq has occurred in part because Americans have recently fought and died there, and may well have to fight there again. The Iraq issue has set the tone for America's continued global engagement following our victory over the Soviets in the cold war. Our Iraq policy has shaped, and will continue to shape, the politics of the Middle East.

The lack of public awareness of the crumbling U.S. position does not derive from a lack of information, but rather from the reluctance to debate the issue shown by those in Washington who are most responsible for shaping foreign policy toward the Middle East. If crafting an effective strategy toward Iraq were to become a national priority, then the policy makers would have to reexamine long-standing beliefs held about Iraqi and Middle Eastern politics. By purporting to possess privileged knowledge and access, such experts have successfully insulated themselves against criticism and forestalled challenges to those long-standing beliefs. A thorough reexamination of their assumptions would expose the policy community to a salutary accountability and would reveal that many of the ideas that led us to war with Iraq persist in defining our regional policies today. It is time we recognized that our Iraqi problem arose not because of incompetent application of ideas but rather because of flawed ideas about the region. A proper analysis of those ideas would unavoidably open a debate on our broader regional policy, its assumptions, and the specialists who have crafted it. For this reason, few within the policy establishment are eager to encourage such an analysis; the issue is too vital to the American people, and there has been too much failure.

This book is particularly critical of the way in which the CIA and other U.S. intelligence agencies have managed the Iraq crisis. In fairness to the staff of these agencies, these individuals devised their plans and conducted them in accordance with directives from leadership at the highest levels of government. The faculty of the universities where these staff people trained have further reenforced the problematic notions of the policy makers. The reader should keep in mind the ultimate cause of the problem—that our Middle East scholarly and policy elite are informed by bad ideas about the region that lead them to bad policies.

As we go to press, dramatic recent events underscore the book's message. On December 16, 1998, the United States launched a series of attacks on Iraq lasting several days. The most serious military challenge to Saddam Hussein since the Persian Gulf War, this campaign shows how we have drifted from the alternative of retreat to that of bombing. But without a clear strategy, such a campaign can only hasten rather than avert our defeat.

Tyranny's Ally is intended to provoke debate not only about our policy but also our policy makers, and about those in our institutions across the country who fail to apply their knowledge about the region to pursue broad American interests.

Acknowledgments

This book is the product of long conversations with many people, and sections and drafts of it were shown to many others. The list of those to whom I am indebted for their patience and insight is a long one, but special names stand out.

First are the two mentors who guided my understanding of the Middle East: Professor Abbas Kelidar and Ahmad Chalabi. Both continually inspire and serve by example to remind me of the great contribution the Arab world offers when its people are accorded intellectual freedom. I am also appreciative of the efforts of Professor Fouad Ajami, another of the Middle East's finest thinkers. Professor Bernard Lewis served as a model of how an outsider can approach the region and care deeply about its people without overlooking warts or evading problems. All of my conversations with him were enlightening and provocative.

A few words about Richard Perle are in order. Since my college days I have held the deepest respect for him, in large part because I credit him with the liberation of many of my family members, who live in the Czech Republic. Richard showed the world how to successfully convert theory into practice in confronting tyranny. It is thus a singular honor for me to have earned his continuing support, suggestions, and encouragement—without which I would neither have arrived at AEI nor been given the opportunity to write. Richard has more than once interrupted meetings to interject, "Let us hear what David has to say," thus purchasing for me attention through the credit of his reputation.

His mind is tough, but his heart is not. That is the chief reason why he attracts such a fiercely loyal group of followers.

The contributions of another AEI scholar, Michael Ledeen, also cannot be overstated. He has sparked in me the drive to reexamine the origins of the Renaissance and the Enlightenment, thus greatly influencing the ideas that inform this book and also prompting my determination to write the next book, *Battle Cry of Tyranny*. Michael has continually reenforced the centrality of promoting freedom and combating tyranny—the principle from which stems so much of modern Western thought. Conversations with him are valued gifts. And thanks are due to Doug Feith, whose inquiring mind kept me thinking about my opinions, whose example propels me to love books, and who always reminds me that peace and principle go hand in hand.

James Woolsey, former director of the CIA, took time from his busy schedule to read the manuscript and give me invaluable advice. By studying his policies as director of the CIA and by listening to that advice, I was greatly assisted in keeping this book pointed in the right direction. Commander Tony Mitchell, a U.S. Navy fellow here at AEI, read numerous drafts of the manuscript, provided me with perspective, and kept me from drifting.

Mark Lagon has done what everyone hopes a true friend will do. He has spent time selflessly, over years, engaging in probing discussions over my latest reflections—always reminding me of the broader context of my views. In the process, he has never allowed me to forget the power of a good idea.

Many of those who read early versions of this book said, "This is a good draft, but it will need a good editor." Fortunately, AEI Press provided me with a great editor in Cheryl Weissman. Her insightful skill and painstaking efforts were invaluable in refining my ideas and converting my lengthy and sometimes confusing language into concise and fluid prose.

I would also like to thank AEI President Chris DeMuth and Vice President David Gerson. In a sharp departure from what I had hitherto experienced in Washington, they made it clear to me that AEI values the autonomy of its scholars. They seek the best and then let them do their best without interference. They thus have provided an ideal environment for research and writing without the burdens of bureaucracy or micromanagement that can impinge on the honesty and unbridled inquiry of thought. I now understand why AEI has become such a powerhouse of original and creative scholarship in so many fields. A note of thanks is also in order for Irving Moskowitz, a gentle man whose generous support of AEI allows me to be here.

A special thanks is due my assistant, Marieke Widmann. Herself a promising future scholar, she assisted in preparing drafts of my report and offered me useful advice. By being one step ahead of me, she frequently kept me out of the trouble an absent-minded and overextended scholar can encounter.

Finally, I would like to thank both my parents, who were always there to give me ideas, listen to my opinions, and provide me with valuable reactions to drafts. And special thanks go to Harold Rhode, who has throughout my career in Washington been a mentor, encouraging me, pushing me forward, acting as my chief advocate around town, and opening the window through which I see the Islamic world. Dozens of people in Washington have benefited from his selfless energy; with his knowledge and his social gift, he effectively holds a portion of this town together.

Freedom and not servitude is the cure of anarchy.

—Edmund Burke
Second Speech on Conciliation with America:
The Thirteen Resolutions, March 22, 1775

1

Introduction

The 1991 war with Iraq constituted the greatest direct military invest-
ment that the United States has ever made in the Middle East. The objective was simple: to remove Saddam Hussein as a threat to the region.
Seven years later, it looks as if that effort may have been squandered.

Seven years after the war, Saddam's regime remains in place. His
power is rising. His diplomatic status is improving, as confidence in
America's leadership among allies erodes and respect for its resolve
among foes wanes. If they are effective, sanctions can deny Saddam's
regime many critical and sensitive technologies and materials, and
they can keep his conventional military forces weak. But sanctions
leak. Inspections, which are crucial to obstructing Saddam's quest for
weapons of mass destruction by exposing and destroying his program,
are stymied. Even military escalation, which occasionally unleashes
considerable force, does little to shore up American prestige or further our interests. The coalition to contain Saddam is rickety and in
danger of scattering. The United States may have won the Persian Gulf
War, but we are rapidly losing the larger contest with Saddam.

The string of crises that occurred in 1997 and 1998 and the hes-
itation with which the United States responded to them should be
viewed in the context of four axioms:

- The political objectives of Saddam's regime will never change.
  Iraq will pursue regional domination and will commit atrocities

against its own people and its neighbors as long as his regime remains in place.

- Sanctions and sporadic attacks might obstruct Saddam's acquisi-
tion of dangerous and long-range weapons and might hamper his
ability to reconstitute Iraq's conventional forces, but by themselves they will never bring down his regime.
- Although they are essential for retarding Iraq's military resurrection, sanctions are a political liability for the United States.
- Recognizing that sanctions cannot be permanently imposed on
Iraq and lacking a plan to overthrow Saddam's regime, many of
our Middle Eastern allies and other, global powers have determined that Saddam will eventually prevail in this conflict. Consequently they have reversed their policy, seeking now to nurture
ties with Baghdad.

Current U.S. policy, even if made more robust by limited military
strikes, must in the long run fail to bring us victory over Saddam and
his regime. The menace from Saddam's Iraq will continue to grow until
the United States starts to direct its threats and blows toward a purpose other than sustaining an already unsustainable status quo. Unless we shift the focus of our policy from one of maintaining sanctions
to one of deposing Saddam, we will be defeated in Iraq.

The focus of this volume, however, is not exclusively on ousting
Saddam. It is on the strategic dynamics of the region. The Iraqi conflict—not simply between Saddam and the United States but also
among Arab nations—has exposed the turbulent undercurrents of Arab
politics and the upheaval that was triggered by Western influence and
the age of modernity. Without appreciating these dynamics, U.S. policy
toward Iraq must necessarily stumble. Our failure to factor these dynamics into our policy making is rooted in decades-old assumptions
about Arab politics. It is leading the United States toward defeat in Iraq.

Strategic Retreat and Failure

In mid-1997 the United States entered an acute crisis with Iraq. Starting in April, Saddam Hussein issued a series of challenges to sanctions, which keep his conventional forces weak, and to the inspections
system, which denies him weapons of mass destruction. At first the
challenges were subtle ones. Iraqi helicopters ferried pilgrims from
the Saudi border so that they could travel home from Mecca during the

annual hajj. But Saddam was emboldened by each unchallenged act of defiance. In September 1997 he threatened to shoot down American U-2 aircraft flying under the UN flag, and he leveled accusations of espionage against U.S. inspectors in the United Nations Special Commission (UNSCOM) inspection teams, who are charged with stripping his regime of all weapons of mass destruction and their means of delivery. Beginning in October 1997 he blocked these teams from visiting key weapons sites.

As the crisis mounted, top officials in President Bill Clinton's administration insisted that Iraq was contained "within a narrow box."[1] With breathtaking confidence, the Clinton administration insisted that since the Persian Gulf War, Saddam had never been weaker and the international coalition to restrain him never tighter. The president himself pointed with pride to the success of his administration's policy toward Iraq at the end of 1997, saying, "We stood strong against a rogue regime in Iraq." Clinton also claimed that U.S. allies were supporting our positions more firmly than ever.[2] Under such conditions, the administration maintained, the policy of containing and outlasting Saddam was a highly reasonable one—both low in risk and low in cost.

But the administration's assertions were unfounded. The United States, not Saddam, was in the "tight box." Already in early November 1997, the administration failed to reestablish unfettered UNSCOM inspections, despite its tough rhetoric promising not to allow Saddam to succeed in his obstruction. In fact, the crisis was resolved only after the Russians brokered a new agreement that changed the constitution of the inspections teams. Within weeks of insisting that the United States would not negotiate with Saddam, the Clinton administration accepted Russia's negotiated settlement. And despite boasts of stronger-than-ever international support, the administration blamed Israel for having weakened the international coalition through its policies—a move that signaled trouble, doubt, and political damage control.[3]

But the October–November 1997 inspections crisis never really ended, of course; rather, it marked the beginning of the U.S. defeat. Saddam was determined to challenge the inspections program that denied him his most cherished assets: weapons of mass terror, to use against his own people and against his neighbors. Dependent as he is on an army of questionable loyalty, these chemical, biological, and even nuclear weapons are the pillars of Saddam's regime. In January 1998, when UNSCOM teams were still being denied entry into biological-weapons facilities and when Iraq announced again that UNSCOM teams were U.S. spies, the United States threatened airstrikes against Iraq unless diplomatic efforts reestablished the status quo ante. We found ourselves isolated. Few allies in the region, let alone nations further afield, lined up to support a threatened U.S. airstrike. Russia's President Boris Yeltsin even hinted several times at escalation to a broader war if the United States were to attack. Our previously enthusiastic ally Saudi Arabia balked, denying the United States the use of its bases from which to strike Iraq. As one American newspaper summed up the American position, "Across the Arab world, the confrontation with Iraq has underscored waning American influence in the region and marked the first step toward bringing Iraq back to the Arab fold."[4] Supported by an unsteady patron, few Muslim states—especially those closest to Iraq, like Jordan, Saudi Arabia, and non-Arab Turkey—could afford to sustain their confrontation with Saddam.

The absence of an end-game scenario troubled Americans as well. The Clinton administration fumbled in explaining its policies to the American public, in large part because the objective of the contemplated attack was only to delay defeat. An attack would merely have delayed the dissolution of sanctions and the rehabilitation of Saddam's weapons-of-mass-destruction program by a few months—at the cost of killing Iraqi "human shields" and risking the lives of American servicemen. The administration's failure to explain its policy—because that policy was insupportable—came to a head in a public forum in Dayton, Ohio, in February 1998. In a televised town hall meeting, the entire senior foreign policy team was stunned to encounter the audience's overwhelming hostility, and it floundered in its response.[5] The crisis and reaction exposed a drifting, defensive U.S. policy and a confident, resurgent Iraq.

Paralyzed by the reception that administration officials received in Dayton and seeking to avoid the appearance of defeat, the United States turned to the United Nations and to Secretary General Kofi Annan to deliver a face-saving agreement to cover our retreat. Despite tough rhetoric about U.S. resolve, the administration accepted the agreement, which diluted the inspections program and opened the door for the termination of sanctions.

In a closed-door meeting with the UN Security Council, Annan referred to UNSCOM inspectors as "cowboys" who, as his remarks were reported, threw their weight around, offended Iraqi sensitivities, and acted irresponsibly.[6] In the same context he also repeated without commenting on a wild Iraqi charge that UN inspectors were tasked to hunt down Saddam rather than to inspect.[7] Although Annan later denied using some of the language reported by those present at the meeting, he said in a later, open press conference that the inspectors "have to handle Iraq and the Iraqis with a certain respect and dignity, and not push their weight around and cause tensions."[8] The agreement he brokered made specific reference to "respecting the sovereignty and territorial integrity of Iraq," echoing his words during a joint press conference with Iraq's deputy prime minister Tariq Aziz. There he said that "UNSCOM inspectors and the UN sanctions should also be sensitive to concerns as to the dignity, security, and sovereignty of Iraq."[9] By accepting the agreement and by applauding Kofi Annan's efforts at his White House reception, the United States effectively assented to the international legitimacy conferred on Saddam by the secretary general. Annan praised Saddam Hussein's "courage, wisdom, flexibility" and called him a man "I can do business with," adding, "I was impressed by his decisiveness."[10]

In the summer of 1998 the Clinton administration found itself isolated on the Iraq problem. Most nations that could potentially be aligned with the United States, such as our Middle Eastern and West European allies, would very much have liked to enjoy the unlimited access to Iraq that the destruction of Saddam's regime would provide. The American people, who once fought to diminish Saddam, would also have liked to see the problem terminated by the destruction of his regime. But both had measured U.S. policy and concluded that it was lacking. And few would follow leaders who could not, or would not, lead.

As a result, Americans were hesitant to reenter a war without the hope that it would resolve the Iraq crisis. Allies, especially those in the region, were wary of provoking Saddam without being certain that this time his regime would be destroyed. They had been encouraged to challenge Saddam before, only to find American support fickle. They believed that Americans would tire of the conflict over the long term, and they feared, reasonably, that they would be left to stand alone against Saddam. Seeing themselves isolated and Iraq's neighbors equivocating, Americans questioned the price of pursuit.

The United States had retreated. We sought at best to create the illusion of maintaining the status quo, while in fact the situation was dynamic and deteriorating. As a result Saddam, rather than the United States, mastered the field, shaping events to realize his own long-term strategic objectives.

Such a quandary demanded concentration, initiative, and intervention from the Clinton administration. But these responses were unlikely to materialize. They could not appear unless there were a long-term strategy for victory—a goal that could be defined only as the overthrow of Saddam. The administration, however, had no such plan.

A Symbol of the Region's Political Malaise

The looming strategic defeat of the United States is especially sweet for Iraq because of the larger, regional struggles in Arab politics. The political undercurrents of the Iraqi conflict, and especially its attending inter-Arab rivalries, reflect the clash of ideas that have been reverberating within Arab and Muslim societies for most of the twentieth century. The region has long been coping with modernity and the influence of Europe. The clash among Arabs to lay claim to Arab identity parallels an ideological clash within the West during this century, which Paul Johnson has termed the "age of modernity"[11] It is a conflict between tradition and revolution, between the politics of humility and the politics of arrogant utopianism.

Iraq has always been important as a regional font of ideas. Baghdad has traditionally had great influence on the region's politics, partly because of geography. Historically known as Mesopotamia, Iraq was a strategic crossroads for millenniums. The Euphrates and Tigris River valleys served as the conduit for all travel between the Levant, Europe, and the eastern Mediterranean, along with their empires, on the one side; the Persian Gulf and Asia, along with their armies, on the other.

When Iraq was not hosting heavy imperial traffic, it served another important function—as a refuge. Situated at the outer and unruly—yet cosmopolitan, double-bordering—edges of two great medieval empires, the Persian and the Byzantine, Iraq was traditionally a haven for the intellectually and religiously freewheeling and for scientifically effervescent communities. Its location afforded Iraq a generous distance from the deadening rigidity and implacable severity imposed by the government at the heart of either empire.[12] During Byzantine times, for example, waves of refugees belonging to dozens of unfortunate early Christian factions getting crushed in internecine struggles fled eastward, to the Euphrates and Tigris River valleys.[13] Having found safety in Iraq, refugees were at leisure to contemplate their defeat and their ideas. Consequently, many of the brilliant minds of medieval Islam, such as al-Farabi, emerged there. The historical flow of refugees, misfits, armies, and money made Mesopotamia a great crucible of ideas. And even today, Iraq boasts one of the most technologically advanced, educated, and urbane populations in the Arab world.

Modern Iraqi politics, however, offers no shining example. In governance and political ideas, it is an abyss. Over the past forty years, thugs have ruled Iraq in the name of Ba'thism. Perhaps as much as 5 percent of its population have died at the party's hands, and at least another 5 percent may have been killed in wars pursuing Ba'thist ambitions. The state of Iraqi politics indicts more than just Iraq's leadership and Iraqi Ba'thism, however. Iraq's malaise reflects a much broader crisis afflicting Arab politics. Saddam Hussein represents the disastrous culmination of the tyrannical republican version of pan-Arabic nationalist governance, which has dominated many Middle Eastern countries since the early 1950s.

The nightmare of Iraqi Ba'thism has forced a vigorous and intellectually active community into exile. Much of this expatriate community, which fled Ba'thism and formed the core of the broad-based Iraqi opposition, has been shaped by bitter experiences with totalitarian tyranny and tantalizing exposure to the West and its ideas—not unlike some of the populations of Central and Eastern Europe. Familiar as they are with the inherent evils of absolute power, many of these exiles are leading the call for greater decentralization and democratization of Iraqi and Arab politics. They challenge not only current Arab despots but also their supporters in the West, who claim exclusive understanding of Arab society. To discover a hope for Iraq we must tap Iraq's exiles, not elements within the Ba'thist regime. We must focus on those outside Iraq who challenge Arab tyranny, rather than those who see the Arab world through the eyes of tyrants and excuse their tyranny.

From Desert Storm to Retreat

The befuddled approach that the United States takes with Iraq—trying successively first to cooperate (1980–1990), then to damage militarily (1991), then to contain (1991–1995), and finally to bring down Saddam through coups and plots (1995–1996)—is motivated by one central and overarching misjudgment. Our current policy regards the Iraq problem as one limited to the ambitions of a single man who can be pressured or replaced. But the problem is not restricted to the monstrosity of Saddam's character. Rather, it is the inherent threat and violence of tyrannical government itself. The United States has dealt with Iraq as it has traditionally dealt with the region—by ignoring the bond between internal tyranny and external aggression. Not the tyrant alone, but tyranny itself must be challenged. And such challenge implies a change in Iraq far broader than an assassination.

U.S. policy toward Iraq should be based on ideas as well as on geostrategic considerations. The crisis over Iraq presents an urgent opportunity for the United States to signal a new policy message to the Middle East region: that despotism, the greatest, most irreconcilable threat the West can face, is unacceptable to us. To adopt such a policy, however, would represent a significant departure from our decades-long approach to the region. The purpose of this book is to illuminate the necessity for such a departure.

2

The Spent Storm—Illusions and Betrayal since the Gulf War

The current crisis with Saddam did not begin in October 1997, but in mid-1995, when the United States abandoned a "safe-haven" zone established for the Kurds and halted our support for the main umbrella Iraqi opposition organization, the Iraqi National Congress (INC).

Although Iraq has commanded a great deal of U.S. foreign policy attention since the end of the cold war, developments within Iraq—especially efforts among Iraqis and successive American administrations to depose Saddam—have remained obscure. Media reporting would suggest that the United States has restricted itself to a policy of containment on Iraq, but that is not entirely true. For some of the seven years since the war, Iraqi nationals and American administrations have tried to rid Iraq of Saddam. In fact, by the summer of 1995 these efforts had endangered and nearly terminated Saddam's regime. He was closer than he had ever been, since the massive revolt of 1991, to his final defeat.

But these efforts all ended in failure, because of the choices made by policy makers at key moments. As a result, in 1998 Saddam stood poised to shove the United States into a free fall—with respect to Iraq and to the Middle East generally. What policy led to the success of 1995, and what policy replaced it, leading to the failures of 1997–1998? To understand why these attempts have failed and to establish a correct strategy to remove Saddam, it is important to review what was tried and what has happened since the end of the Persian Gulf War in March 1991.

The Revolt of 1991

As the war with Iraq ended in 1991, President George Bush urged the Iraqi people to take matters into their own hands and depose Saddam.[1] Iraqis heeded the exhortation and revolted. Fourteen of Iraq's eighteen provinces engaged in open rebellion, and those few troops loyal to Saddam ran out of ammunition. Saddam's own chief of military intelligence estimated the troops' supplies to be a meager two days' worth.[2] It was of course to be expected that the nation's majority Shi'ites and minority (and largely non-Arab) Kurds would revolt; unexpectedly, many of the minority Sunni Arabs, who hold exclusive power in Iraq, also revolted. Within weeks of the gulf war, about 70 percent of Iraq's population were no longer under Saddam's control. Saddam seemed to be at the end of his days.

But the revolution was not to be: the United States lifted ceasefire restrictions on Saddam's helicopter force and allowed it to crush the revolt. We did so for a few reasons. First, we feared that the breakup of Iraq would disrupt the already fragile stability of the Arab state system. Second, we feared that such a breakup, the establishment of a Shi'ite entity in part of Iraq, or internal anarchy would invite Iran's intervention. Third, the United States believed that a coup led by Saddam's top colonels offered an alternative that addressed all these concerns. In fact, as the revolt was underway, one of Saddam's senior diplomats in Moscow, Minaf Hassan al-Takriti, "defected" to Saudi Arabia. There he reported that his brother, al-Hakim Hassan al-Takriti, the head of Iraq's helicopter forces, was in the midst of planning such a coup. The United States was told (and believed) that the coup was imminent—but was being delayed, for cause. Purportedly, the military elite feared both the humiliation that the army would face following the dissolution of Iraq and the general anarchy it would create. Such chaos would lead to Shi'ite or Kurdish revenge killings of the Sunni elite—the very people who formed the top echelon of Saddam's army, from whom the coup was to come.

To encourage the coup, U.S. representatives met with the leadership of Saddam's army in Safwan, Iraq, in March 1991. They signaled the generals, and hence Saddam, that he could employ air power—the only weapon he had left—to crush the revolt, even though the Iraqis had not themselves requested permission to make armed helicopter flights. The U.S. national security adviser, General Brent Scowcroft, observed, "I frankly wished [the uprising] hadn't happened. I envisioned a postwar government being a military government. . . . It's the colonel with the brigade patrolling his palace that's going to get him [Saddam] if someone gets him."[3] The United States clearly envisioned a potential coup—which we hoped would transfer power smoothly, with minimal violence, maintaining seamless control in Iraq—as a source of stability, an enterprise worthy of strong encouragement. As a CIA deputy said at the end of the gulf war, "Our policy is to get rid of Saddam Hussein, not his regime."[4]

The revolt was duly crushed. In the following three weeks, a quarter million Shi'ites were killed by Saddam's regime. The Kurds, who had been the target of Iraqi gas attacks before the gulf war and had lost approximately 200,000 in these unspeakable massacres, fled the anticipated onslaught. But there was no coup. Minaf Hassan al-Takriti was a decoy, and his brother lives in happy retirement in Baghdad, a hero of Saddam's regime.

The millions of Kurds who fled moved into northern Iraq's mountains and beyond, into neighboring countries. The huge refugee flow presented the United States with a humanitarian challenge and threatened the internal stability of other regional countries. We intervened in northern Iraq, launching Operation Provide Comfort to create a safe haven in which Kurdish refugees were promised assistance and protection from Saddam's regime, *even by using ground forces if necessary.* On April 16, 1991, President Bush described the policy as follows:

> Many Kurds have good reason to fear for their safety if they return to Iraq. And let me reassure them that adequate security will be provided at these temporary sites by U.S., British, and French air and ground forces, again consistent with the UN Security Council Resolution 688. . . . Our long-term objective remains the same—for Iraqi Kurds and, indeed, for all Iraqi refugees, wherever they are, to return home and live in peace, free from oppression, free to live their lives.

This operation was not strictly a humanitarian gesture; it was hoped that creating a safe haven in Iraq would stem the tide of refugees flowing into Turkey or Iran.[5]

MAP OF IRAQ, SHOWING THE NORTHERN SAFE HAVEN

From 1991 on, the United States guaranteed this safe haven. Protecting the zone demonstrated, to both our friends and our foes in the region, U.S. resilience and commitment. Through the zone's existence, the United States established the principle that opponents of Saddam's regime could find safety and solace from Saddam's vengeance. Further, the zone signified that resistance to Saddam would not imply certain death but rather would establish the dissidents' credentials with the global power determined to change the regime in Iraq.

By late 1992 the area began to acquire broader importance. Not only were the fleeing Kurds secured, but so were others who opposed the regime. At the same time, the zone was slowly transforming from a haven for refugees and dissidents into a springboard for insurgency. Most of the major anti-Saddam opposition factions of Iraq, including Shi'ites from southern Iraq, congregated in October 1992 in the northern Iraqi city of Salaheddin to create the Iraqi National Congress. The purpose of the INC was to coordinate opposition activities and to provide leadership around which the opposition, and perhaps the future government of Iraq, could assemble. The Central Intelligence Agency also supported the pro-American INC, in the hope that the organization would manage a (primarily) propaganda war against Saddam's regime.

When the Clinton administration took office in 1993, the new CIA director, James Woolsey, continued to support the INC, even though some within the agency persistently urged him to support a Sunni-based coup instead. The INC moved quickly to organize its insurgency, using northern Iraq as its base. Their plan for overthrowing Saddam depended on one key assumption: the same terror that compelled Iraqis into submission also drove them quietly to hate their leader. As a result, the Iraqi army was believed to be the Achilles' heel of the regime. The money that Saddam had long been collecting, from smuggling and from sanctions-defying exports of oil, had been funneled toward benefiting his personal welfare and building weapons of mass destruction. But his conventional army was languishing, posing a far smaller threat than it did on the eve of war in 1990.

Observers believed that this languishing army, weakened by sanctions and beset by extremely low morale, was largely unfaithful and well capable of surrendering, indeed defecting, to a far smaller Iraqi opposition army. Strong evidence recommended this view. During the gulf war, few Iraqis fought for Saddam; almost all surrendered en masse, without a fight, when American soldiers confronted them.

At the time we assumed that this reaction resulted from the fatigue induced by relentless, heavy bombing. But the March 1991 revolt demonstrated that Saddam enjoyed little popular support within his country. Iraqis were willing to fight and die, but only to oppose, not to support, Saddam. In 1998, Iraqis remained discreetly disaffected with Saddam. Despite severe penalties against deserters, almost one-third of Iraq's army was absent without leave, as were 17 percent of the officers of the elite Iraqi Republican Guard Corps.[6] As during the gulf war, then, it appeared to remain likely that many of Iraq's soldiers and officers would surrender their units intact, rather than fight if challenged. Thus even a ragtag army enjoying open Western support could challenge the Iraqi army if its strategy were to subvert, rather than to destroy, Saddam's forces.

Building, Then Betraying the INC

From 1992 until 1995, the INC amassed an insurgent army in northern Iraq to challenge Saddam and launch guerrilla attacks on his regime. Strong and clearly worded guarantees from the highest levels of the U.S. government encouraged and protected the INC. By early 1995 the transformation of northern Iraq was complete. It was no longer just a safe haven for the Kurds, but was also a base from which dissidents, defectors, and army deserters could launch a war on Saddam's reign of terror.

In early March 1995 the Iraqi National Congress fielded its army and attacked Saddam's forces, to test its suspicion that most of Iraq's army would readily surrender. As the INC leader expressed it, "We wanted Saddam to go on full alert, to try to fight back, and see that his units would not fight for him."[7] As part of the operation, the U.S. government's representatives in northern Iraq had gone to some lengths to ensure that the INC operation would be launched under favorable conditions. These lengths even included sending a message to the Iranians, through the INC, to mobilize some of their forces near Iraq's border—ostensibly to deal with the Mujahedin al-Khalq, a group operating from Iraq (under Saddam's control) against the Iranian regime. In reality, this mobilization was intended to force Saddam to divert some of his forces to the Iranian border, away from the northern safe-haven zone.[8]

As the INC attacked, Iraqi units and their commanding officers indeed defected without fighting. As expected, northern Iraq became a sanctuary for thousands of defecting Iraqi soldiers willing to fight to overturn their leader.

At the moment of the insurrection's success, however, the United States withdrew its support. Some members of the CIA and the Clinton administration had envisioned the INC as a public relations tool to weaken and distract the regime; they had never intended it to create a real insurgency or to perform in the main theater of operations in the plan to get rid of Saddam. Some feared that if the rebellion went awry it could embroil the United States directly; others held that it could lead to the dissolution of Iraq, or to a broad-based revolution and consequent anarchy, if it succeeded. At any rate, all agreed that the INC's activity threatened the Sunni core of the current regime in Baghdad, from which they hoped a coup would still come. As a result, the White House ordered the CIA to withdraw its support from the attack and told the Kurdish leaders bluntly, "The United States will not support this operation militarily or in any other way."[9] The CIA agent responsible for the plan was also ordered to tell the INC, "If you go ahead [with your operation], it will be without U.S. involvement or support."[10] In an extraordinary departure from policy, the order came not from the CIA's director, John Deutch, but from the White House itself.[11]

Kurdish factions, from whose territory the insurgency was launched, were stunned by America's betrayal. They feared that Saddam would interpret the U.S. abandonment as a green light for an attack on the Kurds, the prospects of which evoked chilling memories and terror. Consequently, the Kurdish Democratic Party (KDP), from whose territory the incursions had been launched, withdrew its support for the insurgency. That faction's concern for maintaining a safe haven took precedence over its hopes to make the zone a springboard for opposition. The most damaging consequence of America's desertion of the Iraqi National Congress was the wedge it drove between INC and Kurdish interests—calling into question the INC's very reason for existence.

The betrayal also undermined the INC's efforts to mediate among rival Kurdish factions. For Iraqis opposed to Saddam, survival is tenuous. One of the strengths of the INC was its role as middle man: it delivered American protection and served as the conduit for influence to Washington. Abandoned, the INC lost its utility, and the Kurdish factions had to scurry to make deals with whomever they could to secure their short-term survival.

For the remainder of 1995 and the first half of 1996, the Clinton administration attempted to explain its betrayal of the INC as a prudent move designed to avoid embroiling the United States in the internal politics of a fractured, ineffective organization. In the words of one administration official at the time, "They [the opposition] are really more gnats and mosquitoes to Saddam rather than anything serious."[12] Another key U.S. official derided the INC as existing only because it was on life support from the United States, saying, "These guys are a feckless bunch who couldn't hold up a 7-Eleven."[13] In the spring of 1998, the accusation of the INC's inability to maintain unity within its ranks reappeared as one of the harshest criticisms against it, especially among administration officials responsible for policy in 1995. In short, those who betrayed the INC cited the consequences of their act of betrayal as an ex post facto vindication of that betrayal.

As time passed, the administration came to argue deconstructively that the INC was never, in fact, betrayed. Beginning in mid-1997, administration officials asserted that the INC's claims of American support were untrue; that at most, perhaps, some renegade, "cowboy" CIA operatives might have overstepped their authority, but the United States had never officially authorized support for an insurgency. In the words of Assistant Secretary of State Robert Pelletreau, "It sounded to me that there might have been a cowboy out there exceeding his instructions."[14] Leading administration supporters in Congress strove to present the case that there was no betrayal, only misguided, inflated expectations among the INC's leaders.[15]

The evidence to the contrary is overwhelming. John Deutch, the CIA's director at the time, later admitted that no CIA agents were operating on their own in northern Iraq, as Pelletreau had suggested.[16] Regarding inflated expectations, both the Kurds in northern Iraq and the INC were told explicitly that the United States would defend their safe haven from an attack by Saddam. "I am the envoy of the U.S. government, and the representative of the U.S. president, and we have decided to change the regime in Baghdad," the CIA agent said to one Kurdish leader.[17] When asked whether the United States would support the Kurds with air support from retaliation, he unequivocally answered "yes."[18]

Nor were statements of support emanating only from the CIA or only from one quarter of the U.S. government. On August 4, 1993, Vice President Al Gore wrote in the name of President Clinton to the INC president, Ahmad Chalabi, that the INC was "spokesperson for millions," that the United States affirmed its "solid commitment" to "your struggle," and that the administration pledged that U.S. officials "will not turn our backs."[19] The director of Near East–South Asian Affairs at the National Security Council at the time, Martin Indyk, summarized U.S. policy as follows:

> Our purpose is deliberate: it is to establish clearly and unequivocally that the current regime in Iraq is a criminal regime, beyond the pale of international society and, in our judgment, irredeemable. We are also providing stronger backing for the Iraqi National Congress as a democratic alternative to the Saddam Hussein regime. The INC has succeeded in broadening its base to encompass representatives of all three major communities in Iraq, Sunni, Shi'ite, and Kurd. . . . We are now urging others in the region to accord the INC the recognition and support it deserves.[20]

The State Department also supported this policy: at the same time as Indyk made this statement, the assistant secretary for Near East Affairs testified before Congress that "President Clinton reaffirmed the continuity of our policy toward Iraq. . . . We support the work of the opposition Iraqi National Congress."[21]

The highest levels of the U.S. government had clearly supported the insurrection that they subsequently abandoned. Despite the subsequent Clinton administration disclaimers, the Iraqi National Congress built an insurgency under the assumption that the United States supported the destruction of Saddam's regime and supported the INC as the tool to bring it about. The INC also, with cause, expected American military support in defending the safe haven from Saddam's revenge. By forsaking our commitments, we undermined American credibility and reputation for dependability among our friends—the effects of which loss in stature were to reverberate in our consequent Iraqi dealings. Feckless nations find few loyal allies over the long run.

Saddam's Long and Precarious Summer of 1995

Iraqis under Saddam's control were slower than the Kurds to perceive the implications of the U.S. abandonment of the INC. In fact, even though the campaign was halted, the initial successes of the insurgency sent shock waves among the Sunnis in Baghdad and throughout Iraq. But the threat of rebellion did not provoke a fear of Kurdish or Shi'ite revenge among these Sunnis, as had been forecast by those Iraq watchers who had sought to foster a coup; rather, it encouraged their open resistance to Saddam's regime. As a result, the summer of 1995 became the most precarious moment for that regime, as it teetered not only in northern Iraq but internally as well, within its core Sunni population.

The first sign of wobbling was a massive revolt that erupted from April to June in 1995 within one of the largest Sunni tribes in Iraq, the Dulaym. The millions-strong Dulaymi tribe, which has branches in Jordan, Syria, and even Israel, was one of the few broadly based, loyal holdouts at the core of Saddam's regime. Its members could be found throughout Saddam's security services, in the elite Republican Guards Corps, and even in Saddam's inner circle of protection, the Special Republican Guards. So loyal had the Dulaymi traditionally been to the Ba'thist regime that the al-Anbar province, in which was located Ramadi, the seat of the tribe's leadership, was generally referred to as the "white governate"—an allusion to the White Russians who remained loyal to the czar even after his fall.

The proximate cause of the Dulaymi revolt was an incident that typified the indiscriminate brutality of Saddam's rule. In 1994 Saddam's son Uday Hussein raped the daughter of a high-ranking air force officer from this loyal tribe, who in turn sought redress for the crime from General Muhammad Madhlum al-Dulaymi. Together the two men complained to Saddam about Uday's crime—and they were promptly arrested. The general was later released, and some months later he conspired to plot a revolt with other air force and Republican Guard officers from the Dulaymi tribe and from another Sunni tribe, the Jibaris. These officers were in contact with the INC and conveyed their willingness to join forces with the insurgency effort, at one point even meeting secretly with CIA agents in the north.[22] In November 1994 Saddam arrested General Muhammad Madhlum al-Dulaymi and several other Dulaymi sheiks for treason. Protective of their own, the Dulaymi elite sent a contingent from Ramadi to Baghdad on a mission to beg Saddam to return the general to his family. In April 1995 Saddam promised to do so. He returned the general to his family—in pieces. Saddam also executed the accompanying sheiks.

The humiliating savagery with which Saddam dismissed this tribe triggered riots in May 1995 that escalated into open revolt, killing hundreds. When the Dulaymi tribesmen killed the pro-Saddam governor of the province, Saddam ordered a Republican Guard unit to crush the revolt brutally. The officer refused, thus allowing the revolt to expand. Saddam sent his son Qusay to Ramadi with a special force, called Saddam's Fedayeen. When Qusay arrived, he first killed the disobedient local Republican Guard commander and then proceeded over the following weeks to crush the revolt.

Saddam's troubles in Ramadi were still not over. When he appointed General Iyad al-Rawi, a prominent member of another loyalist tribe, to replace the murdered governor of al-Anbar province, al-Rawi refused and was arrested. It was clear that Saddam's ferocity in crushing one Sunni tribe shook the confidence of other, previously loyal Sunni tribes who had believed they were immune from the regime's terror.

Nor had Saddam completely quelled the Dulaymi uprising. A new, tribally based opposition movement officially formed on June 8, 1995, at first called the Armed Dulaymi Tribe's Sons Movement. A second round of fighting erupted in mid-June, triggered by the actions of a relative of General Muhammad Madhlum al-Dulaymi. With the support of a Republican Guard unit he attacked a key military and broadcasting facility, along with a jail holding many imprisoned dissidents, in Abu Ghraib, a western suburb of Baghdad. The general's kinsman hoped to free some of his incarcerated tribesmen and to use the captured radio station to declare a general insurrection.

Fighting soon broke out along the entire corridor between Abu Ghraib and Ramadi, and further west toward the Syrian border, as two other important Sunni tribes joined the insurrection, the Albu Nimr and the Shammar. With the inclusion of these other tribes, the Armed Dulaymi Tribe's Sons Movement expanded and was renamed the Supreme Leadership Council of the Union of Iraqi Tribes. On June 19, 1995, the leadership of this movement called publicly for an alliance with the INC, from which they sought assistance. Saddam exploited his advantage of having little threat from the north, thanks to the obliging American curtailment of the INC insurgency. He thus could focus the majority of his forces on crushing this uprising—which he accomplished by the end of June. One can only wonder what might have happened had the Dulaymi revolt occurred in the context of a continuing INC advance from northern Iraq.

But the apparent implosion in Baghdad that had been sparked by the INC successes and the Dulaymi revolt lurched Saddam with another surprise: the humiliating defection of his son-in-law, Hussein Kamal, to Jordan in August 1995. The defection, along with the Dulaymi revolt, exposed the narrowness of Saddam's support base—even among the Sunnis, who had the most to lose by the regime's collapse.

The international community sensed that Saddam's reign was poised for collapse. In the spring of 1995 Russia seemed almost to be coordinating its policies with Iraq's, and it agitated for relief from the strict sanctions against Iraq. But by late summer Russia and France began to voice the need for Saddam to "come clean" on weapons programs before there could be any loosening of the pressure. The two nations were hedging their bets, on the assumption that Saddam's days were numbered.

The Embrace of the *Wifaq*

Despite encouraging signs from every direction, the United States continued to move to abandon the INC and northern Iraq. Behind this abandonment lay our hope that the government in Iraq could be changed through a silver-bullet coup (a covert action) rather than an insurgency (an overt policy). "Pressure came down from the top for a quick kill—for a coup on a deadline," said one CIA officer working in the Iraqi Operations Group.[23] In late 1994, in part under Britain's encouragement, the CIA's London office began to work with questionable defectors within the INC who promised they could deliver a coup.[24] At the center of this effort was General Adnan Nuri. The CIA instructed Nuri to remain in the INC—and to keep the London CIA office informed about its activities.[25]

The CIA quietly disbanded its Iraqi Operations Group late in 1994. In place of the veterans working with the INC the agency established a "special channel," compartmentalized operation to manage contacts with General Nuri. The CIA agents who had been working with the INC were told to stay away from this operation. The special channel's purpose was to work with former army officers who claimed to be in touch with currently serving officers in Iraq, to prepare a coup that would take place before the U.S. elections of 1996.[26] It is not clear whether such contacts had the support of James Woolsey, the director of the CIA at the time, since he was already on the verge of leaving the government. They did, however, have the support of the Department of State, as the following interview reveals:

> *Robert Pelletreau, assistant secretary of state for Near Eastern affairs*: "Frankly, a number of people believed that the

only way you were going to succeed in unseating the existing regime was through an internal military coup against it."

Peter Jennings, ABC News: "Were you one of those
people?"

Robert Pelletreau: "Yeah, pretty much."[27]

On the eve of the INC's offensive from northern Iraq in early
1995, after Woolsey's departure from the CIA, the State Department's
contacts with these defectors accelerated and superseded its efforts to
support the INC broad-based insurgency. The Clinton administration
had chosen to pursue a clandestine coup rather than an overt rebellion, and the new director of the CIA instructed his agency to set
"milestones" for achieving this.

But the CIA operatives in northern Iraq were unaware that the
contacts with the Ba'thist defectors had already effected a policy shift,
so they proceeded to plan the March 4, 1995, attack as they had been
charged to do for years.[28] On the eve of the attack, General Nuri flew
to Washington to derail the insurgency effort. He warned darkly that
the INC was trying to draw the U.S. military into a direct confrontation with Saddam.[29] Apparently, top officials in the White House, specifically National Security Adviser Anthony Lake, became skittish
and ordered the insurgency's offensive to a halt as it was about to be
launched. The administration feared enmeshing itself in a new war
and believed that a rebellion could jeopardize the favored coup strategy. It was too late; the revolt had already been launched—successfully.

Ironically, the success of the insurrection strategy—which in
part had encouraged the Dulaymi revolt and Hussein Kamal's defection—seemed further to validate the arguments of those who had
maintained that Iraq's salvation would come from conspiracies within
Saddam's inner, Sunni circle. Kamal's defection exposed the rickety
nature of Saddam's regime and thus boosted clandestine plans to have
high-ranking Iraqi defectors assassinate or depose Saddam. If some
insiders so close to Saddam were willing to risk their lives by defecting, then surely others might take the risk to assassinate him, American policy makers thought. Kamal's defection also sparked a hope that
he would provide the names of other insiders with whom one could
conspire. Suddenly, the INC's insurgency seemed not only superflu-
ous, but a distraction.

Paradoxically, Kamal's defection tempted the United States to embrace a policy based on the effects of a strategy we were moving to abandon. The temptation proved irresistible. Although the United States was mistrustful of Hussein Kamal himself,[30] Kamal's flight laid the groundwork for a new strategy to topple Saddam—a strategy based on penetrating the core of his regime through Ba'thist defectors in Jordan and in London. At first this plan took the form of supporting Kamal's efforts in Jordan to build a cadre of other high-ranking defectors from Saddam's military that he would head, to be called the High Council for Iraq's Salvation. At one point the United States even favored releasing some of Iraq's frozen assets to fund the activities of this new organization surrounding Kamal.[31]

Meanwhile, King Hussein of Jordan had moved to bring down Saddam Hussein, but the king remained uneasy with the stream of high-ranking Baghdadi defectors arriving from Saddam's inner sanctum—many of whom he regarded as double agents and plants—and with their conspiracies for a military coup. Like the United States, Jordan was particularly wary of Hussein Kamal. King Hussein sought to promote a profound change in Baghdad—he did not want to see merely another Ba'thist regime there. In fact, he saw Ba'thism as the crux of the problem in Iraq, and for this reason he was suspicious of the CIA's penchant for working so closely with Ba'thist defectors. King Hussein preferred to work with the Iraqi National Congress and to pursue a plan of politically organizing Iraq in a fundamentally different way—as a decentralized, "federal" Iraq. In fact, within a month of Kamal's defection, the Jordanians were announcing publicly that they had adopted the INC's vision of ridding Iraq of Saddam and were maintaining contacts with the INC and its member factions, including those in northern Iraq.[32] In September 1995 King Hussein traveled to London to meet with the INC's president, Ahmad Chalabi. He complained to Chalabi that the Americans were seeking an officer to lead a coup, but that he believed no such person existed.[33] By late fall 1995, King Hussein and his brother, Crown Prince Hassan, frequently visited London to discuss and coordinate their policy with the INC-led Iraqi opposition.[34]

Inevitably, the divergent visions held by King Hussein and Hussein Kamal about how to change Iraq soured relations between them. The rift surfaced publicly in February 1996 and contributed to Hussein Kamal's decision to return to Baghdad later that month.[35] King Hussein supported the INC concept of a federal Iraq, while Kamal sought a highly centralized Iraq under his own control.[36] The difference between pursuing a coup and organizing a broad-based insurgency later caused a falling out between the United States and Jordan as well.

Although Hussein Kamal rapidly became a marginal figure for both the United States and Jordan in the months after his defection, his arrival in Amman changed U.S. policy in a number of ways. First, it focused Washington's attention exclusively on Iraq's Sunni population and tribes, for Washington now believed that true change could come only from that Sunni core. Second, because we sought a coup, we concentrated on the traditional ties between the Jordanian-Palestinian leadership class in Jordan and the Sunni elite in Baghdad—as well as on the Jordanian military and intelligence structure's close link with the Iraqi military and intelligence structure. Third, Washington was now reckoning primarily with a Ba'thist exile community in Amman rather than with a more broadly based and representative opposition movement, since high-ranking Ba'thists most easily defected through Jordan. For these and other reasons, the United States shifted its focus from northern Iraq—the geographic springboard for the insurgency—to Jordan, the appropriate site for a coup.[37]

By early 1996 Washington had turned its *exclusive* attention on these Ba'thist defectors, helping their shadowy *Wifaq* movement, also known as the Iraqi National Accord, to hatch a plot for a military coup in Baghdad. To this end, in January 1996 President Clinton authorized $6 million in covert aid to support the *Wifaq*. The most visible among the defectors were General Adnan Nuri in London and Iyad 'Alawi in Jordan. The latter unveiled the existence of the group and announced its creation of an Amman office in a news conference on February 2, 1996. The *Wifaq* also at that time established a military council, which included Nuri, 'Alawi, General Muhammad Abdallah ash-Shahwani, General Bara Najeeb al-Rubayee, Colonel Muhammad 'Ali Ghani, and Salah Omar 'Ali al-Takriti. The insidious al-Takriti was a kinsman of the two aforementioned bearers of that name, who were implicated in the nonexistent coup of 1991, when the United States was duped into permitting Saddam's helicopters to crush the general insurrection. He himself had participated in the 1969 hanging of Iraq's Jewish leadership. Ash-Shahwani was the direct point of contact between the council and the CIA.[38] The purpose of the institutions was openly stated: in the words of 'Alawi, "We think that any uprising should have at its very center the armed forces. . . . We preach a controlled, coordinated military uprising."[39]

The unveiling of the *Wifaq* capped the U.S. policy shift that had been under way since early 1995. 'Alawi's public statement at the press conference was a *Wifaq* "coming out party," and it formalized the year-long CIA contacts with the Ba'thist officers and their coup strategy. It also signaled to the potential coup plotters in Baghdad, whose participation the *Wifaq* promised it could deliver, that the United States backed them fully and that they should step forward and display their courage.

Jordan acceded to American pressure, some of it reportedly from President Clinton himself, and allowed itself to become the regional center for the CIA's efforts to overthrow Saddam. King Hussein allowed the *Wifaq* to conduct business, but he refused to endorse the *Wifaq* publicly in its plan to create a new opposition structure that would replace the INC and destroy Saddam. He instead gave the organization his official support as a "political organization" only.[40]

Quietly, however, while still uneasy with the *Wifaq*, Jordan did allow a base to be set up in eastern Iraq, near al-Azraq, to accept refugees and to serve as cover for the *Wifaq's* military planning. This base became the focal point for a covertly planned *Wifaq* coup. Throughout the spring and early summer of 1996, a constant stream flowed from Iraq to Jordan of Ba'thist defectors, some of whom the INC warned were probably double agents sent by Saddam. One of the highest-ranking of these defectors, a man who was rapidly integrated into the *Wifaq* despite the INC's and King Hussein's grave reservations, was Saddam's former chief of staff, General Nazar Khazraji.[41]

The conspiracy planned by the *Wifaq* never materialized. Both the INC and the Jordanians had warned the United States that the *Wifaq* functioned like the Soviet KGB "trust" organization—a front created by the Soviets in the 1920s and 1930s to lure their enemies into a fraudulent opposition movement, from which they could control and eventually kill them. The INC had good reasons for its suspicions. Earlier, the Bush administration had dismissed the *Wifaq* precisely because it believed that Saddam had infiltrated the organization,[42] and subsequently there came compelling evidence: on October 31, 1995, a bomb tore apart INC headquarters in northern Iraq, killing twenty-nine people. Later, investigators discovered that the bomb had been planted by *Wifaq* operatives, most probably at the behest of Saddam. Yet when the INC offered to give CIA officers in London the results of their internal investigation of the bombing, the CIA declined the offer. The findings of the INC included important information that would have helped the CIA uncover the double agents operating within the *Wifaq*. Moreover, one of the *Wifaq*'s bomb makers announced publicly on a videotape in March 1996 that the *Wifaq*'s leaders had ordered him, again at Saddam's behest, to kill Ahmad Chalabi, the president of the INC.[43] Despite these warning sirens, the CIA continued to direct all its support toward the *Wifaq*, at the expense of the INC and the northern safe haven.

The CIA's efforts climaxed in spectacular failure in July 1996, when an Iraqi intelligence officer located in Baghdad contacted the CIA's station chief—over captured CIA communications equipment—and informed him that the Iraqis knew the detailed plans of the coup plot. The Iraqi informed the American that all the Iraqi officers and agents who had been involved in the plot had been rounded up and executed.[44] Some reports place the number executed that week in the hundreds.[45] Gloating to the CIA station chief in Amman, the Iraqi told the Americans to pack their bags and go home.[46] By the summer of 1996, the United States was left with neither coup nor insurgency. We continued, however, to bankroll and work with the *Wifaq* rather than the INC.

The Balkanization of Northern Iraq

Not only were U.S. efforts to oust Saddam by a coup in disarray by mid-1996, but so was the situation in northern Iraq. As the United States focused on the *Wifaq*, our abandonment of the north devastated INC efforts to mediate among feuding Kurds. We also created a political vacuum in northern Iraq, which Iraq's neighbors exploited by intervening in intra-Kurdish rivalries.

The Iraqi opposition had not always had difficulty keeping the Kurds together. The apex of Kurdish cooperation occurred during and immediately following the 1991 uprising. It lasted as long as the Kurds viewed the United States and the INC as the keys to their partisan survival, forces with whom it was worth currying favor. But the increasing withdrawal of American interest in their plight and a lack of momentum in the anti-Saddam initiative eventually led to a resurgence of their infighting. At about the same time as Kamal defected, the United States worked with the INC to mediate an agreement among brawling Kurdish factions in northern Iraq. Under the agreement, signed in Dublin, the INC was to monitor the cease-fire and the United States was to provide approximately $1 million to the INC to maintain a separation force between the two factions. The United States promised to deliver and disburse this aid through the INC in seven separate meetings over the ensuing months. The assistance never came, because after Kamal's defection the maintenance of the northern Iraqi safe haven ceased to be a priority.

In spurning the INC and forsaking our promises under the Dublin agreement, the United States not only further encouraged Kurdish factions to ignore the INC and resume fighting but also signaled the beginning of our disengagement from northern Iraq. Iraq's neighbors interpreted both moves as signs of U.S. exhaustion and strategic inattentiveness.

The vacuum in northern Iraq soon invited the attention of those countries most anxious to diminish U.S. power in the region. In particular, Iran and Syria moved to extend their influence, and even presence, in northern Iraq. The vacuum left the Kurds to scramble for whatever protector they could find—placing Syria and Iran in strong positions. By late 1995, for example, the Patriotic Union of Kurdistan (PUK) had been forced to operate under Iranian tutelage.

The absence of an American response to Syria and Iran's aggressive moves confirmed the U.S. disengagement. The Iranians, insidiously fueling tensions among the Kurds, magnanimously presented themselves as the mediators of these tensions. Yet instead of condemning the Iranians and Syrians for their transparent ploys to assert dominance, American officials at one point actually welcomed Iran's interference in the zone, as a potential aid in mollifying Kurdish rivalries. Thus we further undermined INC efforts in this direction. By June 1996, Iranian Islamic Revolutionary Guard forces were operating in northern Iraq, pursuing one of the local Iraqi Kurdish factions, the KDP. By failing to help the INC to restore a balance between the two warring Kurdish factions, and especially by failing to challenge the Iranian intervention that greatly fueled the conflict, the United States signaled its abandonment of the zone almost entirely by the summer of 1996.

The U.S. abandonment of the safe haven highlighted for Saddam the power vacuum that the north had become and placed the KDP faction in a desperate situation—either it had to ally itself with Saddam or it would face annihilation at the hands of Iran. Such a vacuum and an opportunity were sure to invite Saddam's attentions.

Saddam's Reentry into Northern Iraq

The crisis peaked in late summer, 1996. King Hussein's efforts to undermine Saddam over the previous year had effectively threatened Saddam. The INC operations conducted in March 1995 had revealed the vulnerability of Saddam's army. In 1995, the two greatest challenges to his regime—the INC in northern Iraq and the UN weapons inspections program—were as formidable as they ever would be.

But by late summer 1996, Saddam was ready to respond to the INC threat. First he had to bully King Hussein, demonstrating to him that the close ties between the Jordanian and Iraqi elite classes could be tapped as easily by Saddam's brutal regime as by Jordanian intelligence. According to the Jordanian government, in August 1996 Saddam fomented riots in a number of Jordanian cities—including the worst in seven years in Kerak—by exploiting his strong ties among Palestinians to derail Jordan's Hashemite option for Iraq.

By mid-1996, it was clear to Saddam that he had successfully compromised the CIA's plot to oust him. He had watched the United States unwittingly but effectively dismantle the menace posed to his regime by northern Iraq, by our abandonment of the INC. Saddam now saw an opportunity to seize the initiative, and he began to reverse the strategic predicament in which he had found himself since the end of the Persian Gulf War. Recognizing the importance of demonstrating his strength to dispel any presumptions that his regime was crumbling, Saddam invaded the northern safe-haven zone. On August 30, with the assistance of the desperate KDP, Saddam's forces entered Irbil, where the INC kept its headquarters, striking a sharp blow against the INC and capturing hundreds of its officers. During the invasion, the United States scurried to evacuate thousands of INC men to Guam, but we did nothing to reestablish the northern safe haven.

Before Saddam's invasion of northern Iraq, Kurdish leaders had contacted the United States to warn that an attack loomed. They had sought assurances that we would stand by our promise to protect the safe haven. Assistant Secretary of State for Near Eastern Affairs Robert Pelletreau had informed the Kurdish leaders that we clearly warned Saddam that he would suffer serious consequences and a strong response were he to enter northern Iraq. The Kurds understood this response as a security guarantee.

But U.S. policy had changed: the safe haven had been reduced to a strictly humanitarian issue. It affected neither U.S. prestige nor U.S. strategy. As Secretary of Defense William Perry said, "Our interest in the Kurds [in northern Iraq] is not a vital national security interest. It's a humanitarian interest. . . . But our vital interests are in the south."[47] As a result, the United States sent a few missiles against insubstantial targets in southern, rather than northern, Iraq and extended the southern no-fly zone northward to the 33rd parallel; but Saddam's invasion of the north stood without real challenge or response. By late 1996 little remained of President Bush's commitment to northern Iraq, whereby the United States would protect the zone from Saddam by ground and air power. In early 1997 Turkey, feeling the pressure of its neighbors' interventions in northern Iraq and observing the anarchy reigning there, also entered the safe haven, to root out Kurdish PKK terrorists. By late 1997 the United States no longer even enforced the northern no-fly zone. America had ceased to be a player in northern Iraq, and as a result the region had become completely "Balkanized."

By late 1997 the U.S. effort to oust Saddam through a coup or conspiracy was in shambles—as was the Hashemite initiative, upon which the United States had foisted the *Wifaq* and its Sunni Ba'thist plots. King Hussein of Jordan, having gone far out on a limb in deferring to the U.S. government's judgment by supporting the *Wifaq* over the INC, was humiliated and despairing. Consequently, he had little choice but to seek his peace with all those among whom he had lately picked a losing fight—Saddam, Assad, Arafat, and Iran's mullahs.

The Clinton administration revised its rhetoric to justify its retreat from northern Iraq, arguing that the zone had never been a vital U.S. interest and thus the collapse of the safe haven was neither a real retreat nor any indication of U.S. policy. Bizarrely, the administration argued that the collapse of northern Iraq vindicated U.S. policy. Attributing Saddam's reentry into northern Iraq and the collapse of the safe haven to the INC's inability to maintain the Kurdish cease-fire, the administration sought to confirm the wisdom of its decision to abandon the INC. In reality, of course, the administration had debilitated the INC through its betrayal—and then audaciously pointed to the organization's diminished stature as retroactive justification for that betrayal.

But despite the Clinton administration's insistence that policy had not changed, the contradictory evidence was overwhelming. The United States was in retreat.

The abandonment of the INC and of northern Iraq, as well as the embrace of the *Wifaq*, began a year-long process that transmuted Saddam's near collapse into the dissolution of U.S. policy toward Iraq. In the spring of 1996, while the State Department confidently maintained that its Iraq policy was "one huge success," that policy was actually on the eve of a humiliating defeat.[48] By late 1997 the Clinton administration had coined a new, benign term for its retreat from northern Iraq: *deconflictualization*. It was a sorry euphemism for retreat: the implication was, since conflict is bad, deconflictualization must be good.

The switch to supporting the *Wifaq* over the INC, which roughly coincided with the departure of James Woolsey from the CIA, marked the fulcrum of the transition of American policy from near victory to retreat. It was the climax of a policy that countenanced betrayal, that was suffused with illusion. The ill-fated U.S. embrace of an imaginary coup strategy left the INC dangling and the United States tarnished. We did not recommend ourselves as a worthy ally for anyone who was concerned with survival.

Challenging UNSCOM and Sanctions

Having witnessed the removal of one of the two greatest threats to his power, the INC in northern Iraq, Saddam moved quickly to address the other—the UNSCOM inspections regime. UNSCOM challenged not only Saddam's ambitions but his very survival. He knew well that his control depended on terror, not popular support. And his authority rested atop a heavily armed, embittered society. As a result, he devised an asset of control—directed first against his own people—that did not require broad-based support: chemical and biological weapons. The terror these weapons instilled, along with his proven willingness to use them, were instrumental in cowing his countrymen into quiet submission and threatening revenge against his foreign enemies. But UNSCOM threatened this vital asset of control.

The lack of American concern over the developing power vacuum in northern Iraq paved the way for a broader decline in the U.S. engagement in the area. The result of this decline, as admitted by the director of the CIA, was that by the fall of 1996 Saddam Hussein was gaining rather than losing strength.[49] Our European allies also noted this development and, believing that Saddam might well prevail in the long run, some of them pragmatically began to resume ties with the Iraqi regime.[50] In the words of one European ally: "What is the structure; what is the goal? The United States does not seem as deeply engaged as before, and where it is engaged, it seems unsure."[51] By June 1996 Saddam began brazenly to harass and obstruct UNSCOM teams, prompting some harsh statements from UNSCOM chairman Rolf Ekeus and the passage of UN Security Council Resolution 1115. Saddam blatantly violated the southern no-fly zone with missile deployments and with helicopter flights, starting in mid-1997. By late 1997, he in effect terminated the UNSCOM inspections regime by barring American participants, by tampering with monitoring equipment, and by threatening U.S. aircraft that were taking part in monitoring efforts to support the UNSCOM mission. And in early 1998 Saddam declared numerous sites, especially presidential palaces and Revolutionary Guard bases, to be off-limits to inspectors. Events in February 1998 emphasized America's retreat. Only months after insisting that Iraq's obligations under the UNSCOM inspections regime were nonnegotiable, the United States welcomed a UN-negotiated agreement to end a U.S.-Iraqi standoff. The agreement in effect provided Iraq with the cover to stymie an effective inspections regime.

The most critical controls on Iraq, which even before the February 1998 agreement were enforced only nominally, were leaking. Saddam's Iraq was cut off neither from foreign exchange (it sold black-market oil) nor from materials to rebuild its military industries. Syria and Iraq quietly reopened their border for unmonitored trade and perhaps for oil transfers, and reports alleged that French companies signed massive contingency oil deals with Saddam's regime.[52] Such agreements helped confirm Saddam's claims to legitimacy and reflected international reliance on his longevity. The international community clearly anticipated that Saddam would outlast the sanctions program and would prevail as the sole interlocutor over the long term for negotiating with Iraq.

Tailspin: The Summer of 1998

For years most Americans respectfully accepted their bewilderment with the subtle, intricate nature of U.S. policy toward Iraq, and so they remained oblivious to the actuality of surrender and collapse of the U.S. position. In the summer of 1998, however, that actuality became publicly obvious. An Op-Ed in the *Washington Times* stated simply, "The Clinton administration's Iraq policy lies in shambles."[53]

Three events in particular revealed the breadth of the continuing defeat. First, a June 1998 U.S. Army testing lab report confirmed that Iraq was hiding its weapons of mass destruction program and accomplishments—this time, its successful adaptation of VX nerve gas for use on SCUD warheads. Second, the *Washington Post* revealed on August 14 that the United States had intervened with UNSCOM, directing the delay or cancellation of inspections that might embarrass or provoke Saddam Hussein—an act that prompted the resignation of Scott Ritter, one of UNSCOM's most diligent and effective inspectors. Third, in testimony to the House International Affairs Committee on September 15, 1998, Assistant Secretary of State for Near Eastern Affairs Martin Indyk outlined a new strategy. Rumors of this policy change had circulated but had been denied by the Clinton administration since March; arrantly abandoning credibility, Indyk presented the policy as one of continuity.

The VX story erupted on June 23, after the Iraqi National Congress leaked it to the *Washington Post:* the Clinton administration possessed but was quietly ignoring the alarming results of a U.S. Army test of SCUD warhead fragments discovered during an UNSCOM inspection earlier in the year. Lab tests conducted on June 10 at the Aberdeen Proving Ground confirmed that the SCUD samples were doused in stabilized, weapon-ready VX nerve gas. On June 16 the head of UNSCOM, Richard Butler, reported to the UN Security Council that Iraq had formally, vigorously denied having such weaponized warheads. But the U.S. Army test results revealed Iraq's blatant deception and violation of the terms of UN Security Council Resolution 687—the basis for the 1991 cease-fire and for the 1998 Annan agreement. Butler accused Iraq of concealing information and obstructing the inspections; Iraq and the United Nations had launched on a new round of confrontations.[54]

Concomitant with the UNSCOM chief's accusation that Iraq was "holding back data" and so obstructing the inspections process, Secretary of State Madeleine Albright released a contradictory statement—arguably, it was technically correct, but it was thoroughly misleading. Albright suggested that Iraq was living up to its commitments under the Annan agreement and UNSC Resolution 687: "To date, inspections under this agreement have gone smoothly."[55] On June 24, President Clinton himself reported to Congress that Iraq was continuing to fulfill its requirements under the terms of the February 23 Annan-Aziz Memorandum of Understanding and UNSC Resolution 1154. To his credit, the president reserved the possibility that Saddam might eventually cheat again.[56] But effectively, despite mounting evidence that the Annan-Aziz agreement had been abrogated, the Clinton administration continued to behave as if it were still being upheld. Unwilling to be pushed into another confrontation and a more robust policy, the administration took no action on the terrible information it had held since June 10.

Frustrated with this inertia, the INC leaked the unclassified report to the *Washington Post* late on June 22. Even before giving the story to the press, however, the INC sent a copy to the Senate leadership, which in turn issued the following decisive letter to President Clinton on June 22:

> We are deeply troubled by the apparent failure of the United States to fully support the work of UNSCOM at a time when its efforts to verify Iraqi compliance . . . are under assault. We are no longer surprised by efforts of some members of the Security Council to sweep evidence of Iraqi violations under the rug. However, we are now receiving reports alleging that the United States has allowed itself to become complicit in such efforts. We have been informed, for example, that the United States has not responded to attacks on the integrity of U.S.-provided intelligence information. . . . Even more troubling, we have heard that the United States has acquiesced in the suspension of challenge inspections. . . , and that the United States no longer is urging UNSCOM to present strong evidence of Iraqi violations to the Security Council.[57]

The congressional statement "that the United States has not responded to attacks on the integrity of U.S.-provided intelligence information" referred to an exchange that had taken place earlier that month, during a UN Security Council meeting. Without encountering any resistance from the U.S. delegate, the French delegate dismissed the credibility of intelligence used by UNSCOM on the rationale that it had originated with the United States—implying that we simply fabricate our claims to serve our own interests. Indeed, even after the public revelation of the Aberdeen report, State Department spokesman James Rubin took great pains to insist that the circumstance was an "apparent" rather than a certain violation by Iraq, thus himself discrediting the accuracy of the U.S. Army lab tests.[58] Rubin's remarks lent credence to the French disparagement of our credibility. As a result, Congress sent an ominous letter to the State Department demanding to see all cables pertaining to the Iraq issue on the dates surrounding the incident, to determine whether the administration had directed its UN delegate to avoid confronting the French when they impugned the U.S. intelligence services.

The congressional claim that the United States was no longer urging UNSCOM to present strong evidence of Iraqi violations to the Security Council was exposed the next day by the publication of the aforementioned *Washington Post* article. On June 25 Congress, already disturbed by the administration's handling of Iraq, passed HJ Resolution 125, declaring:

> Whereas on June 24, 1998, UNSCOM director Richard Butler presented information to the UN Security Council indicating clearly that Iraq, in direct contradiction of information provided to UNSCOM, weaponized the nerve agent VX; whereas Iraq's continuing weapons of mass destruction programs threaten vital United States interests and international peace and security; and whereas the United States has existing authority to defend United States interests in the Persian Gulf region; now therefore be it resolved by the Senate and House of Representatives of the United States of America in Congress assembled, that the government of Iraq is in material and unacceptable breach of its international obligations, and therefore, the President of the United States is urged to act accordingly.

The second charge leveled in the June 22 congressional letter—"that the United States had acquiesced in the suspension of challenge inspections"—was proved true a few months later, joltingly calling public attention to the breadth of the U.S. retreat in Iraq. The revelation came that the United States was actually obstructing inspections; it was quickly followed by the resignation of William Scott Ritter, one of UNSCOM's most capable inspectors.

President Clinton had promised back in February, following the Annan-Aziz agreement, "I believe if [Iraq] does not keep its word this time, everyone would understand that then the United States and hopefully all of our allies would have the unilateral right to respond."[59] James Rubin the next day had added that "military force would ensue" immediately if Iraq came into breach.[60] A week later, Clinton had threatened the "severest consequences" if Iraq did not uphold the agreement. On August 3, Saddam announced that he would no longer cooperate with UNSCOM, blatantly abrogating the Annan-Aziz agreement.

Despite the president's promises, the United States struggled to avoid a confrontation in August. Our behavior confirmed a policy shift rumored to have occurred since March. The new strategy dictated that force would no longer be used to enforce the inspections regime.

When Saddam threatened on August 3 to terminate inspections, the Clinton administration, rather than acknowledge the collapse of the Annan-Aziz agreement, cravenly moved to crush an UNSCOM inspection planned for August 5. Our State Department judged that this imminent inspection had provoked Saddam into confrontation. To defuse the crisis, Madeleine Albright summoned Richard Butler on August 4 (he flew to Bahrain to receive her call) and instructed him to cancel the August 5 inspection. Butler postponed the inspection until August 10 and flew to New York to consult with the UN Security Council. In the meantime, National Security Adviser Sandy Berger viewed CNN footage showing Scott Ritter arriving at the UNSCOM compound on August 4 and concluded that Ritter was trying to initiate an inspection in contravention of Albright's expressed wishes. Berger frantically called the U.S. mission in New York and ordered that Ritter be confined to the UNSCOM compound and avoid being seen by the press. On August 8 Ritter was ordered to leave Iraq immediately.[61] It was a contest of wills; determined as Saddam Hussein was to provoke a confrontation, the United States was equally determined to retreat from one.

The administration's efforts to keep the lid on the boiling pot were in vain. Saddam's August 3 termination of inspections exposed and escalated the crisis, previously known only to a few attentive senators and representatives. Furtive efforts made to avoid confrontation now became public knowledge, illuminating the stark contrast with the administration's bold rhetoric.

In the first sign of the coming public storm, the *London Times* bluntly reported on August 10 that "the United States is so eager to avoid a new military confrontation with Iraq that it has blocked more United Nations weapons this year than Baghdad."[62] The storm erupted in full force across the Atlantic when the *Washington Post* reported on August 14 that the United States was dissuading UNSCOM from conducting searches that could trigger a new round of conflict with Saddam.[63]

In the following days, the administration labored simultaneously and contradictorily to explain that its policy had not changed, that it did not tell UNSCOM how to do its job, and that it had broader considerations to consider in advising UNSCOM to hold back. While Albright was insisting there was no interference, her deputy, Thomas Pickering, said that merely listing the interferences "misses reams of context" in which these decisions to interfere were made.[64] In fact, as late as August 17 the administration still employed the harshest rhetoric to threaten Iraq.

Less than two weeks after the first stories appeared about U.S. attempts to halt some inspections, UNSCOM inspector and Gulf War hero Scott Ritter resigned, saying, "Iraq is being allowed to redefine the terms of the UN cease-fire resolution that stopped the gulf war. I fought in that war and cannot be part of that. It would mean that hundreds of Americans would have died in vain."[65]

After Ritter's resignation the full extent of the retreat on inspections became even more apparent. The *Washington Post* reported that the interventions were not merely recent but in fact dated back almost a year, despite the administration's harsh and resolute rhetoric against Saddam's obstructionism and promises of "severe consequences."[66]

Throughout the summer the administration continued vehemently to insist that there had been no shift in U.S. policy, that we would respond forcefully to a violation of the Annan-Aziz agreement. After Ritter's resignation the line was subtly changed: the shift was only minor and tactical. Thus the State Department acknowledged and began to explain its new policy. The events of August further incensed Congress, which called for a series of hearings on Iraq to be held by both the Senate and the House of Representatives. The point man for the administration was Martin Indyk, who gave the clearest explanation of U.S. policy on September 15 in testimony before the House Committee on International Affairs, chaired by Benjamin Gilman. Indyk outlined the constraints under which the administration labored, and he appealed to Congress to understand and refrain from criticism. The constraints described were indeed harsh and stark:

- There is no international support for any use of force to enforce the inspections regime.
- Any use of force short of invading and conquering Baghdad will isolate the United States and, therefore, undermine sanctions.
- Without the option of using force, the United States has to rely exclusively on diplomacy to maintain sanctions, even if this comes at the expense of a robust inspections regime.

In short, the policy of the United States had changed fundamentally. Rather than using confrontations over inspections to emphasize the importance of maintaining sanctions, the administration now retreated from inspections. The State Department hoped that such demonstrated accommodation of the "international consensus" would shore up that consensus behind sanctions.

Indyk's appeal for understanding and patience and his revelations about the strict limitations under which the Clinton administration was laboring begs an important issue: the limitations were of the administration's own making. Far from meriting praise and admiration for making the best of a bad situation, Clinton's team was responsible for a resounding policy failure.

The limitations tying American hands in 1998 directly followed from policy choices made in 1995. Had a credible force under the INC been supported and enabled to survive in northern Iraq, the United States could have used each confrontation over weapons of mass destruction to further erode Saddam's domestic authority. For example, we could have extended the no-fly zone into the desert areas west of Ramadi in Iraq and built no-drive zones as well—areas where no heavy equipment of any sort could enter—in southern and western Iraq. Alternatively, we could have provided the INC's forces with effective anti-tank equipment so that they themselves could enforce a no-drive zone.

Were these measures in place, then each crisis provoked by Saddam would have further diminished his power by denying him more territory and the people and resources in it. Our military strikes could have been directed at conventional forces rather than targeting useless, cleaned-out sites of weapons of mass destruction, with human shields sitting atop them. Our strikes in response to Saddam's provocations could have been used to erode his military potential against the insurgents by specifically targeting those troops most loyal to Saddam and closest to the liberated areas of Iraq. Such strikes would also encourage less loyal soldiers to defect rather than face attack, and they would help the INC extend the territory under its control by further expanding the no-drive and no-fly zones.

We could have presented Saddam with a stark choice, rather than enabling him to present one to us; each act he undertook to preserve and pursue his weapons-of-mass-destruction programs would have enlarged the INC and diminished his conventional and material assets. And the territory of the INC would steadily have expanded, denying

Saddam access to people and to oil. He would thus have had less money with which to pursue his grisly programs, and nothing to offer those who wished to help him violate the sanctions. Moreover, sensing Saddam's predicament, more international actors would hesitate to alienate the United States for fear that we might indeed emerge victorious in the contest. The likelihood of this occurring is slim indeed as of the autumn of 1998.

In sum, crises over inspections could have been used to advance a coherent strategy to remove Saddam without using American ground troops. Having betrayed the INC, however, the United States was left with no options other than the equally unappealing ones of occupying Baghdad or struggling to maintain an international consensus, to sustain increasingly enfeebled sanctions.

Another *Wifaq*-Led Coup Attempt?

The only apparent glimmer of hope in this bleak state of affairs came when information was leaked to the *Wall Street Journal* on July 17 that the administration had an active plan to topple Saddam's regime. According to reports, this plan was larger in scale than anything attempted by the Clinton administration before, and it included broader political-military—or, covert and overt—scope.[67]

As the summer wore on, however, this "new" plan was unveiled as merely an old, failed plan on a larger scale. In fact, the plan appeared to be a variant of one formulated by Daniel Byman and Ken Pollack at the Washington Institute for Near East Policy, known as the "undermine strategy."[68] Its objective is stated thus:

> The "undermine" option uses the Iraqi opposition to destabilize Saddam Hussein's regime and thereby create the circumstances in which he could be overthrown. . . . The policy assumes that anyone in power in Baghdad would represent a major improvement because any successor would be less aggressive and brutal than Saddam. Although it may be preferable that the opposition take power rather than a henchman of Saddam, insisting on an opposition victory will be difficult and will make a coup or assassination less likely.[69]

In other words, the opposition should be encouraged to run an insurgency, and the various groups opposing Saddam, such as the Kurds, Shi'ites, and others, should be unified. The role of the opposition, however, is merely to create enough instability within Iraq as to encourage a coup. This notion represents a return to the policy choice taken in late 1994 and early 1995 with respect to the INC.

The contours of how the administration planned to put this plan into operation became apparent during the latter part of the summer. Part of the effort entailed creating, as Congress demanded, a Radio Free Iraq. Appointed to oversee this program was David Newton, former diplomat to Iraq in the 1980s and ambassador to Yemen in the 1990s—and one of the architects of the policies that led the United States to the gulf war and to the abandonment of the Kurds and the INC in 1995.

And true to historical pattern, the administration returned to the *Wifaq*, not the INC, to spearhead opposition efforts. As the *Wall Street Journal* noted in its expose, one of the steps taken to unite the Iraqi opposition was to hold conferences in the Hague for exiled opposition groups.[70] Such a conference was indeed held in early September—organized by the *Wifaq*.

Most disturbing of all in the light of our past mistakes, the administration was undermining and paralyzing an effective policy for the third time. Like the 1991 uprising and the 1995 INC offensive, any potential insurgency was being abortively sacrificed to clear the way for an elusive coup. According to the *Wall Street Journal*, this attempt, like the previous ones, appeared to be timed to take place just before the next presidential elections.[71] Poised to inspect certain highly suspected properties and facilities connected with Saddam's closest associates, UNSCOM was suddenly betrayed and these most effective inspections prevented by the United States. Clearly we sought both to avert a desperately feared confrontation with Saddam and to facilitate the coup plan—which, ironically, relied on Saddam's closest associates.[72] Thus the Clinton administration obstructed inspections and provoked Scott Ritter's resignation to pursue the same strategy that had originally led the United States into the 1998 policy impasse.

Regional Implications

The U.S. administration's efforts to overthrow Saddam, specifically those focused on fomenting a coup or an assassination, had all failed. U.S. allies in these efforts had gone their own ways, driven by self-preservation and by lost confidence in American leadership. Jordan felt increasingly isolated and threatened by Saddam and was economically damaged. As a result, the country sought to improve relations with Baghdad, in part with France's encouragement.[73] Other regional allies, including Saudi Arabia, Kuwait, and Turkey, sensed this trend and hesitated in lending their support to U.S. efforts to maintain inspections and to uphold containment. Few will follow into battle a leader whose resolve to lead and fight is doubtful.

These events signaled America's strategic retreat in Iraq. By maintaining his initiative against the United States, Saddam forced a change in the status quo such that little would remain of the restrictions placed on him in the first half-decade after the gulf war. The harder he pushed, the weaker the international community's will grew to sustain what restrictions remained. Judging that Saddam could well prevail over the long run, that community considered it unwise to expect the sanctions regime to outlast and defeat Saddam. U.S. policy was reduced to little more than a defensive enterprise to sustain what few sanctions were left, or at least to retard their further erosion. The Clinton administration's insistence that Saddam was contained, or was being kept "in a tight box," rang hollow. Developments in the field simply did not support American verbal bravado.

The strategic defeat of the U.S. policy on Iraq will have far-reaching consequences. As the gulf war signaled America's determination to remain globally engaged, so the resurrection of Saddam could be read as a signal of America's retreat into isolationism. The world's leaders, both those who benefit from and those who are obstructed by America's power and purpose, will draw the appropriate conclusions and craft the appropriate policies. We will lose allies and embolden enemies.

The Current Policy of Silver-Bullet Coups

U.S. policy toward Iraq consistently fails because it favors the covert pursuit of a coup rather than overt support for an insurgency. The preference for a coup is rooted in the following assumptions, which generally inform American policy toward the region:

- Only a strong, heavy-handed central government can hold Iraq together as a nation and provide an element of stability.
- Iraq's external aggressiveness—toward both its neighbors and the United States—reflects Saddam's, rather than Ba'thism's, nature.

- A real change in Iraq will be possible only if we encourage a rift among elements of the narrow Sunni clique surrounding Saddam. Broad internal pressure in Iraq against the current upper classes forces them to "circle the wagons" around Saddam, reducing the chances for such change. To threaten despots only serves to strengthen them.
- An uncontrolled revolt will lead to a Shi'ite fundamentalist regime allied with Iran.
- United within the INC framework, the INC, Kurdish, and Shi'ite efforts to overthrow Saddam will lead to the breakup of Iraq and to its eventual submission to its neighbors, including Iran.

A coup, assassination, and subsequent installation in Baghdad of a secular Sunni military officer close to Saddam would satisfactorily meet all the aforementioned considerations. Thus, current U.S. policy focuses on containing Iraq and waiting until a player or clique within the regime steps forward to remove Saddam. And periodically the United States attempts more actively to foment a silver-bullet coup.

U.S. policy makers who support the coup option also enjoy broad support from outside the government. For example, Washington's most respected Middle East research institute, the Washington Institute for Near East Policy, has suggested that the United States announce a general amnesty to all but the highest-ranking members of Saddam's regime—a position that evinces hope for change in Iraq occurring internally, within the current Ba'thist system.[74]

The attempt to organize a coup requires the support of Saddam's closest associates. Since 1991, the advocates of such conspiracies have argued that the broad-based internal upheaval in the nation and the separation of the Shi'ite and Kurdish areas into northern and southern safe havens have humiliated Iraq's Sunni military establishment and thus forced it to support Saddam. Such unrest, it is argued, raises the specter of anti-Sunni revenge and deters action among the Sunni officers close to Saddam. The military can focus on overthrowing Saddam only after it is cleansed of the tarnish of this humiliation and relieved of internal—especially Shi'ite or Kurdish—unrest. For these reasons, the United States allowed Saddam's generals to crush an uprising that had spread throughout most of Iraq in March 1991. In addition, the United States not only lost interest in maintaining the northern safe haven in 1995–1996; we actually began to see the INC efforts as a threat.

U.S. policy toward Iraq is not unique; Washington's preference for a coup over a broad-based revolution illustrates a deeper theme underlying U.S. policy in the Middle East. In contrast with policies in other areas, the United States has traditionally aimed its blows in the region at individual tyrants rather than at the institution of tyranny, hoping that friendly tyrants might bring stability. We do this because we consider that the greatest threats to U.S. interests and regional peace are the violence and fractionalization that result from internal political instability.

Yet the Iraqi National Congress maintains that the tyrannical nature of governance in Iraq itself is at the core of the Iraqi problem. The INC argues that the violence in the region does not stem from the region's fractionalization or from the lack of internal political cohesiveness within Middle Eastern nations. Rather, the root of the violence is a century-old radical attack on the Arab world's traditional elite; it is the grip of centralized, totalitarian power and despotism. An attack on tyranny should be the focal point of U.S. policy toward the region, the INC warns. An insurgency in Iraq provides an opportunity not only to rid Iraq of Saddam but to rid the Arab world at large of totalitarian despots such as Saddam. For Ba'thism itself, not Saddam alone, is the problem. A coup would merely install another Ba'thist officer who is close to Saddam and who would inevitably fail to solve the problems of Iraq.

But U.S. officials have never accepted this INC view, because they believe that such a scenario could lead to the disintegration of Iraq, as foreshadowed by the INC's inability to hold together a coalition. Thus, the question remains: What brings stability? Is it managed chaos, as the INC argues, or firm, centralized control, as current U.S. officials and most Middle East specialists claim?

3

Nations at War with Themselves and Their Neighbors

Why is the United States so averse to supporting the broad-based Iraqi opposition that nearly defeated Saddam, choosing instead to embrace coup plots, the consistent results of which have been spectacular and humiliating failure?

Iraq is a problem because it is a totalitarian tyranny. Such tyranny is, by its very nature, violent, aggressive, and rabidly anti-Western. To deal effectively with Iraq, the United States must strike not only at the tyrant but at the institution of tyranny in Iraq. Ba'thism is a prominent example of it, but the problem is common to all forms of pan-Arabic nationalism. The United States has long tolerated and even deferred to despotic Middle Eastern regimes for two reasons: first, to preserve "stability," and second, to assert our anti-imperialist credentials by displaying "sensitivity" to the most revolutionary sentiments in the Arab world. Consequently, U.S. policy has turned a blind eye to the inherently subversive, destabilizing, and anti-American character of Ba'thist despotism. We have refused to support the Iraqi National Congress, persevering instead with our elusive coup strategy. Simply put, that choice is responsible for the U.S. failure to bring down Saddam Hussein.

To be effective, policy must begin with an appreciation of the political character of the nation in focus. Iraq's tyranny reflects its own idiosyncratic version of pan-Arabic nationalism, a Middle Eastern movement conceptually derived from the wracking upheavals of modern European history. The Middle East has not been immune to the effects of aberrant Western thought that led to angry and devastatingly violent revolution in Europe. The *Zeitgeist* that infected the European intelligentsia in the second half of the nineteenth century continued to inform the politics of the twentieth—a politics dominated by unrestrainedly ambitious men who arrogantly profess to the power of changing human nature.

America's strategy toward the Middle East must confront pan-Arabic nationalism, particularly Ba'thism. Until such politics—rather than politicians—is defeated, anti-Americanism and violence will infect the region.

Is Tyranny a Path to Stability or to Anarchy?

Assumption: Only a strong, heavy-handed central government can hold Iraq together as a nation and provide stability to the region.

Over the past three decades, it has become increasingly fashionable in the West to argue that a centralized, intrusive state that subordinates local or individual forms of identity and loyalty is a force for stability. Only the state can overpower the resilient institutions and patterns that make local politics so fractured and "primitive." One of the greatest threats to the Western world, the argument contends, can emerge from the dissolution of Arab states and the reemergence of primordial social entities—tribes, families, villages, regions, sects, and ethnic groups. These social elements purportedly compete with the state for the people's loyalty. Hence, pan-Arabic nationalism is seen as a positive force that challenges the power of religion and faction and transforms traditional into progressive societies. Once modernized, such states can become building blocks for regional stability. And it takes muscular measures of persuasion to smelt the diverse communities of artificially cobbled nations like Iraq and Syria into integrated nation-states. Over time, by the sheer momentum of the power of the state and the prevalence of its institutions, even an artificially created nation can assume an air of permanence and legitimacy.[1]

Many highly respected theorists in Middle Eastern studies note the instability inherent in externally assembled states—an instability seemingly remediable by expansive state authority. These political scientists recognize the fundamental problem for the citizens of Arab states—competing loyalties between those to the regime and those to traditional touchstones such as family, tribe, and sect. When the state administration's power expands to permeate most aspects of society and to elicit people's dependency for their welfare, the theorists argue, the balance tilts for the better. The nation, synonymous with the state, then firmly grips a people's identity and allegiance.[2] And an unfettered Arab state apparatus—indeed, *only* the state apparatus—can transform primitive societies and artificial nations into homogenous entities, thereby securing for the United States regional stability.[3]

Some theorists recognize that this model of social transformation bears costs. Lisa Anderson, one of the most respected Middle Eastern political theorists, concedes this:

> That state patriotism has not completely eclipsed alternate identities reflects both the heterogeneity of the societies encompassed by the states and, perhaps more important, the fact that the state-directed social transformation of the state itself is implicated in the damage such transformation inevitably entails for old social classes, norms, and networks. Social change is not cost-free, and those who bear the cost can be expected to identify and oppose its source.[4]

Champions of the notion that the state is the effective engine of development and modernization interpret the danger to which Anderson refers as cause to strengthen the state's power to crush such heterogeneity and entrenched opposition. In short, they side with the region's totalitarians against the old regional elite and its more local, diffused leadership, despite the totalitarians' despotism and anti-Americanism. For example, a 1963 Council on Foreign Relations study group, some members of which eventually became senior officials in subsequent administrations, produced a report on the rise of the Ba'th in Syria and of Nasser in Egypt. The study dismisses the belief in the universal human aspiration for freedom and obsequiously applauds pan-Arabic nationalism as the appropriate political culture for the Arabs. Its portrayal of Nasser and his fellow Arab nationalist dictators is particularly smarmy; it celebrates their repressiveness as a noble virtue:

> Nasser's Arab nationalist foreign policies represent valid historical forces. . . . He has captured the mood and seen

the demands of the times. . . . Nasser and nationalists of similar stripe throughout the Arab world are honest and trustworthy in their dedication to national goals. . . . Their conduct is less influenced by self-interest than is that of holders of power in the traditional governments in that part of the world. . . . The United States . . . cannot deal with them only to the extent that they meet our standards of respectability.[5]

The authors of the study betray a shockingly patronizing and derogatory attitude toward the political maturity and potential of Arabs universally. The underlying assumption evident in the report is that the West's emphasis on freedom is inappropriate for the Middle East, where politics are exotic and primitive, rooted in tribalism and local forms of identity—indeed, all forms of political decentralization. The effort to overcome such a primitive nature excuses, if not requires, the excesses of radical despotism:

The authoritarian practices characteristic of Nasser's government, and particularly his management and control of the press and public opinion, are often cited as fundamental weaknesses. But . . . they must be related to the stage of political and social development in which the Arabs find themselves, and to the outside interference to which they are subjected.

Egregiously, the council report bluntly warns that the United States should not succumb to the fallacy of treating friends better than enemies![6] Hostile despots should be sycophantically placated while friendly Arab states, leaders, and movements should be sacrificed; clinging to them could ensnare the United States in tumult and could damage our prestige, were these allies to fall or lose. And defeat is inevitable for these friendly regimes, the council concludes, because the currents of history favor "progressive" forces.[7] Such thinking, articulated in 1963, seems still to inform Iraq policy today. Our fear of entanglement on behalf of an insurgency first paralyzed and eventually shut down our support for that insurgency.

This Council on Foreign Relations report is a window into the world of ideas that has informed policy makers on the Middle East for decades. It was a product not of obscure academicians far removed from the corridors of power and policy making in Washington, but of the mainstream policy establishment. Its message was clear:

- revolution is inevitable in the Arab world
- its excesses are tolerable as the necessary means of overcoming the traditional and tribal bases of Arab politics
- its repulsiveness and anti-Americanism should not deter America from courting its proponents—at the expense of our friends

Condescendingly, the council generously makes allowance for the Arabs' "stage of development."

Hewing to this philosophy, U.S. regional policy has traditionally tolerated repressive, intrusive, and centralized states in the Middle East as a necessary evil. We have come to view pan-Arabic nationalism as a progressive force in Arab politics, especially when it competes with Islamic fundamentalism. We have accepted Syria's continued occupation of Lebanon and the Palestinian Liberation Organization's human rights abuses in the Palestinian Authority. We also sided with Iraq against Iran in the Iran-Iraq war. And we now favor a Ba'thist military coup in Iraq rather than a dissident-led revolution.

But this focus on stability—and the policies that flow from it—represents a strange deviation from Western tradition. The most highly valued leadership in the Western world is that with the skill to exploit instability. In the business world, few CEOs succeed by exhausting themselves and their companies' assets to maintain the status quo. Effective corporate leadership recognizes that constant change and some chaos are a given. Opportunity and progress are determined by the ability to navigate through disorder and fluidity and to engineer their currents to a company's advantage.

Furthermore, grandiose political efforts to change society radically necessitate absolute power, which attracts ambitious, corrupt, and dangerous men. When the state tears down and rebuilds the people's loyalties, civil society is disrupted. It can then be cynically exploited and left utterly vulnerable to tyranny, which pillages first its own people and then its neighbors. This is hardly a prescription for stability.

Pan-Arabic Nationalism

To comprehend the fecklessness of encouraging a military coup in Iraq, we must first recognize the irreconcilability of the pan-Arabic movement with Western interests.

Pan-Arabic nationalism is an offshoot of the twentieth-century, post-colonial trend to forge new nations around centralized and highly intrusive governments. It gained a burst of energy in the 1930s within a pro-Nazi, anti-British Arab resistance movement. Lacking the power to sustain its empire but seeking to remain in the Middle East, Britain elected to appease the extremist forces in the region, even according them official recognition as predominant actors. The British hoped to mollify opposition to their own continued presence and to co-opt the extremists politically.[8] As the Middle Eastern scholar Elie Kedouri has observed, these efforts created, confirmed, and emboldened extremist movements, rather than harnessing, tarnishing, or undermining their appeal.

Kedouri offers two examples. The first is a 1919 episode involving Britain's colonial rulers in Egypt, Lords Edmund Allenby and Alfred Milner, and a marginal but menacing figure, the former Ottoman officer Saad Zaghlul. This man sought a political role for himself in the post–World War I order by rabble-rousing against the British. Soon after Zaghlul was arrested, Allenby released him from jail in Malta, in a gesture intended to convey largesse and conciliation. Kedouri describes how Allenby and Milner's efforts at appeasement backfired, elevating the stature of this otherwise peripheral figure into something formidable:

> Allenby's action was interpreted as an indication of British weakness and a proof of Zaghlul's strength. Zaghlul could now claim that he was the sole representative and spokesman of the Egyptian people . . . and that the British had willy-nilly to deal with him alone.[9]

As the violence grew in response to Zaghlul's incitement, the British sought desperately to address the grievances that putatively were the cause of the radical leader's popular support. They failed to understand that Zaghlul's power with the people resulted chiefly from the importance the British themselves were investing in him. First the British appointed a member of the Cabinet, Lord Milner, to head a commission to investigate Egyptian grievances. This was a mistake. Zaghlul mobilized his following and joined forces with a secret terrorist organization, then used it to establish a thuggish political apparatus. With intimidation and terror he enforced a boycott of the commission. The British still did not recognize their error, but Milner and his fellow commissioners decided that it would be best for Britain to divest itself of Egypt altogether.

The British wanted to withdraw from Egypt in such a way as to

safeguard their vested interests, and so needed to promote a coopera-
tive leadership there. Astonishingly, they still believed they could co-
opt the fiercely hostile Zaghlul. After Milner's departure, a former
Egyptian minister and personal adviser of Milner's persuaded him to
invite Zaghlul to London for talks. The naïve hope was that Zaghlul
could assist the British by facilitating the negotiation of the treaty. Kedouri describes the effect of this strategy in Egypt:

> Zaghlul hastened to advertise the invitation from the Brit-
> ish Colonial Secretary. . . . This enhanced Zaghlul's stature
> in Egypt enormously. . . . [He] was claiming that he was the
> sole representative of the people. . . . No political figure
> dared to demand anything less than Zaghlul was demand-
> ing.[10]

A second example involves the French in Syria in the 1930s,
when a small, pro-Nazi group managed to dupe the French into crown-
ing them the leaders of Syria. In the late 1920s the National Bloc infiltrated Syria's parliament—not to participate in the orderly pro-
cesses of parliamentary governance, but rather to disrupt them and
subvert France's mandatory authority with "belligerent and spectacular" tactics.[11] Still, the National Bloc failed to command much popular following. In a 1932 election a nonnationalist majority was returned to power, despite the bloc's bullying and coercion. France at
the time was led by a new, left-of-center government that chose to follow Britain's example in Iraq and terminate their mandate.

The French government invited a Syrian delegation to Paris to
participate in treaty negotiations—a delegation that predominantly
consisted of National Bloc members, who baselessly claimed to represent the Syrian people. But the readiness of the French government
to extend a virtual monopoly in negotiations to the National Bloc members invested them with a significant amount of authoritative credibility. In the negotiations the French quickly acceded to all of the bloc's
demands—including the primary one, that an independent Syria become a centralized state ruled from Damascus, under National Bloc
control.

Having secured such a clear victory over the French, the bloc
easily persuaded the Syrian population that it was the recognized force
to contend with. With the shadow of Nazi power cancerously growing
in Europe and the West falteringly retreating from the Middle East, the
National Bloc swept to victory in the Syrian elections of November

1936. This episode was to haunt the British and French in the World War II years.[12]

Paradoxically to British intentions, resistance to Britain was galvanized and its genuine allies unnerved by its appeasement policy. Pan-Arabic nationalist resistance to the British role in the Middle East was the result neither of Britain's identification with Zionism nor of otherwise flawed, "insensitive" policies; rather, it was a fundamental rejection of Britain's presence and everything for which it stood. Placating the revolutionary Arabs thus could do nothing to win them over. Britain's solicitousness instead exposed its unease with its own policies and caused the Arabs to smell retreat. The appeasement policy accelerated Britain's regional expulsion rather than prolonged its regional presence, and it helped bring radical movements to leadership of the Arab world by the late 1950s.

At the same time as pan-Arabic nationalist movements sought to expel the British, they also waged war on traditional Arab society. Nationalistic feelings arose among Arabs during World War I, fueling their revolt against the Ottoman Empire. Patriotism came to be channeled along two distinct paths, however, and the rift between them became profound after the war. The historian of Arab nationalism Bassam Tibi identifies the two camps as, on the one side, the followers of the Hashemite regent Sharif Hussein, ancestor of King Hussein of Jordan; and on the opposing side, the republican, radical, pan-Arabic nationalist movement. Tibi examines the difference between the two:

> Sharif Hussein wished to restore [Mecca and Medina] to their former glory by means of the Arab Revolt and the support of the colonial powers, in order to consolidate the ideological foundations of his rule. While the Syrian Arab nationalists used national revolutionary arguments to justify the uprising, and made the Sharif their leader, the latter interpreted it as an uprising of Islam against Turkish "heretics."[13]

These revolutionary nationalists were the Levantine renditions of the anarchic revolutionaries appearing in Europe in the mid-eighteenth century. They cast a long shadow over the political scene throughout the continent, but most particularly in Russia. Three features distinguished them: anger and destructive nihilism toward the establishment; a conspiratorial quest for absolute power; and the transformation and usurpation of religion into secular form, based either on race

(Nazism) or class (communism). Russian literature at the twilight of the prerevolutionary era addressed these three tendencies, which sought to disguise human arrogance as utopian idealism.

The Revolutionary Spirit in Europe

In *Fathers and Sons,* Ivan Turgenev memorably depicts the clash of values between the insolent and nihilistic character Bazarov and the traditional, establishment figure Nikolai Petrovich. The latter articulates the viewpoint of the prerevolutionary society:

> "We of the older generation think that . . . without principles taken as you say on trust, one cannot move an inch or draw a single breath. . . . Yes, it used to be Hegelians, and now there are these nihilists. We shall see how you manage to exist in a void, in an airless vacuum."[14]

A fictional character from another Turgenev work, Rudin, elaborates on the conservative philosophy:

> "If a man has no firm principles in which he believes, no ground on which he is firmly based, how can he determine the needs, the significance, the future of his people? How can he know what he must do himself?"[15]

What most impressed Turgenev and other Russian writers about the revolutionary *Zeitgeist* was its destructive animus. It targeted deeply held beliefs and values, along with institutions, in a mission to promote truly radical change. And such an ambitious program can be achieved only when all power is concentrated in, all civil society subordinated to the state. Hence the second phenomenon addressed by Russian writers: the conspiratorial quest for power. No one personifies this aspect better than the chilling character Peter Verkhovensky in Fyodor Dostoevsky's *The Devils.* Another of the novel's characters, Nicholas Stavrogin, describes Verkhovensky's modus operandi to Shatov, who naively assumes he can quit the conspiratorial revolutionary society:

> "You changed your views . . . and you wanted to resign. . . . You undertook to carry out their instructions in the hope and condition that it would be their last demand on you and after that they would release you entirely. . . . These gentle-

men have no intention of parting with you. . . . They have many agents, some of whom don't even know that they are in service of the society. You've always been kept under observation. Peter Verkhovensky, by the way, came to settle your business once for all . . . to liquidate you at the first favorable opportunity as one who knows too much and who might inform the authorities."[16]

Dostoevsky illuminates also the third aspect of this revolutionary phenomenon: arrogant utopianism that seeks to destroy and replace all traditions in revolution, rather than to build on tradition through evolution. Describing the ideas animating the younger Peter Verkhovensky, and particularly his fascination with violence and death, the character Kirilov articulates the radical doctrine:

"Full freedom will come only when it makes no difference whether to live or not to live. That's the goal for everybody. . . . [Man's fear of death and love for life is] despicable, and that is where the whole deception lies. . . . Now man is not yet what he will be. A new man will come, happy and proud. To whom it won't matter whether he lives or not. He'll be the new man! He who conquers pain and fear will himself be a new god. . . . He'll be physically transformed. . . . Everyone who desires supreme freedom must dare to kill himself. . . . He who dares to kill himself will be god."[17]

The embrace of a cult of suicide leads inevitably to impassive disregard for human life—and a zest for killing opponents of the creed.

Within a few decades of this novel's publication, Dostoevsky's fictitious characters effectively came to life as Lenin, Stalin, and Trotsky. Their ideas, along with racially based analogous ones in Germany, ravaged Europe. Thus were the Renaissance and the Enlightenment assailed in the twentieth century by a utopian distortion of modernity—a scourge that descended over European politics and then spread to those of the Middle East.

European Influence on Arab Revolutionaries

Such European trends energized Arab radicals. They looked to two common sources—the French Revolution and German political philosopher Johann Fichte—to inform their ideas. A generation after their European counterparts, *fin de siecle* Arab revolutionaries advo-

cated the overturning of society in all its aspects. The constitution of
the Ba'th Party, promulgated in Damascus in 1947, unabashedly proclaimed, "The [Ba'th Party] is revolutionary, since revolution is the
only means to its declared ends. This entails a struggle to destroy co-
lonialism, unite the Arabs, and overthrow the social and political system in the Arab world."[18] They sought to replace local and provincial
loyalties and identities (tribe, family, clan, city, sect, ethnic group, or
political affiliation) with a new, universal, secular, racial, pan-Arabic
identity and centralized authority. Ba'th Party founder Michel 'Aflaq
voices the philosophy in the *Muntalaqat*, the treatise adopted in 1963
by the sixth Pan-Arabic Congress of the Ba'th as the party's ideological manifesto:

> Popular revolutionary democracy is therefore required. Its
> object is to destroy reaction and the bourgeois-feudalist
> framework of democracy. . . . This can only come about with
> revolutionary vanguards leading the popular masses. This
> means centralized democratic powers.[19]

'Aflaq habitually spoke and wrote of "the need for revolution, with all
the connotations of violence and strife with which it abounds."[20] "Progressive" socialism and a new secular-nationalist religion were to replace traditional religion. A centralized and intrusive state was to replace traditional patterns of diffused authority. And the new order
relished conspiracies—both planning them and professing to see them
everywhere. For example, the following is a communique from the
Ba'th Party Organizational Bureau in Syria:

> The Party's answer to the state of ignorance and clannish-
> ness is Arabism. . . . The Party stated from the beginning
> that regionalism, sectarianism, and tribalism were danger-
> ous social diseases to be combated by any method because
> they seriously increased and deepened the fragmentation of
> society. . . . The enemies of the people realized that armed
> conspiracy would only make the Party stronger and more
> determined. . . . Therefore, the imperialist media and Arab
> reactionaries . . . exploited sectarianism, regionalism and
> tribalism as a means to bring an end to the Party. . . . The
> pollution was thus able to seep through into the minds of
> some people and undermine the ideals of many to such an
> extent that they felt no shame or hesitation in dealing with
> the Party's affairs on a sectarian or regional basis. They thus

strayed into the treacherous quagmire of deviation and became, whether they knew it or not, a tool for the fifth column. . . . Such a person should be punished as though he were an enemy of the people.[21]

The main obstacle to such a radical effort in the Arab world more broadly was the Hashemite leadership. These elites were connected not only with traditional Arab society and religion, but also with the colonial nations, whom the Hashemites treated amicably. In the words of one of the pan-Arabic nationalists,

> [The Hashemite] national movement was largely a political movement in the narrow sense; it had no social or humanitarian perspectives. It fought merely for independence. . . . Secondly, it was a right-wing conservative movement . . . monopolised by traditional politicians who were usually either rich feudalists or their agents. They saw their own interests as being the interests of the homeland and excluded workers, peasants and the middle classes. . . . Thirdly, the movement had no confidence in itself or in the nation; hence it was based more on foreign capital than on people, and tended to dance to tunes played in foreign capitals.[22]

Two governments in particular were eventually crafted around Ba'thism, one of the extreme variants of pan-Arabism. An Iraqi revolution expelled the Hashemites in 1958, and by 1968 the country had fallen to the Ba'thists. The Syrian regime was seized by the Ba'thists in 1963. Like the early Russian revolutionaries, Ba'thists drew inspiration from German political thought. As Bassam Tibi notes,

> It was Sati al-Husri who began the tradition of populist Germanophile Arab nationalism. His nationalism was not mystic, fanatic, or fascist, but he laid the foundations for the kind of fanatical nationalism formulated by his disciple, Michel 'Aflaq, which has found expression in the semi-fascist military dictatorship in Iraq and Syria under the aegis of the Ba'th Party.[23]

Pan-Arabic nationalism and Ba'thism are explicit in their goals to combine three ideas: socialism, "Arab awakening," and racial pan-Arabic nationalism. Bassam Tibi describes the ideas of Michel 'Aflaq as follows:

> 'Aflaq resents the individualism of the West and empha-
> sizes the collectivity in a unitary "Arab nation." To be an
> Arab nationalist is not to be an individual, but rather a limb
> of Arab collectivity. . . . 'Aflaq adopted the Islamic concept
> of collectivity of all Muslims united in one *Umma*, but sec-
> ularized it, in confining it to the Arabs viewed to be a na-
> tion in the European sense. In both cases, there is no place
> for the individual.[24]

Regarding the Arab awakening, 'Aflaq wrote:

> The past for which our nation is longing . . . is the time when
> the soul of this nation finds realization. The future . . . which
> must be struggled for . . . can only be that future in which
> the Arab soul is reborn.[25]

The Arabic word *Ba'th* means rebirth, and the name of the party comes
from this tract.

Ironically, it was under the protection of Hashemite Iraq—which
eventually became one of its first victims—that this radical body of
thinkers first established an institutional presence. At the core of the
Iraqi army after World War I stood members of secret societies—the
most powerful of which was the al-'Abd—espousing violent and destructive politics.[26] One group, the support behind the rising Palestinian nationalist leader and mufti Hajj Amin al-Husseini, was linked to
the Iraqi secret societies through Uthman Kamal Haddad.[27] The latter was both the private secretary of the mufti and the primary contact
between Baghdad and the emerging Nazi party in the 1930s.[28]

Eventually an alliance united the pro-Nazi faction in Baghdad
under Rashid 'Ali al-Gaylani with Mufti al-Husseini, who was eventually exiled to Germany, and with the Third Reich. The common
enemy of al-Gaylani and al-Husseini was as much the Hashemite family, which ruled Iraq and some of Palestine, as it was the British. Their
mutual antipathy formed the leading edge of an upheaval within Arab
society that came to be expressed in a global struggle. During World
War II the Hashemites and the British crushed these movements, but
only temporarily; the same officers and figures of the al-'Abd movement resurfaced a decade and a half later, when pan-Arabic nationalists established the Palestinian national movement and swept aside
the Hashemite leadership in Iraq.

The intellectual founder of the Ba'th movement and the teacher of Michel 'Aflaq was Sati al-Husri, who was in Iraq during al-Gaylani's tenure and who was forced to flee to Syria when al-Gaylani's government fell to the Hashemites. Al-Husri became a key figure in Syria's education ministry by 1945, sowing the seeds from which another radical pan-Arabic nationalist movement would eventually sprout.

All these movements sought to effect a radical transformation of Arab society. But they first had to subordinate and eradicate all the institutions, powerful figures, and ideas that stood in their way—to destroy before they could build. Historically, the phenomenon reflects the intrusion, transformation, and integration into the Arab world of turbulent intellectual currents that have swept over the West for two centuries, erupting most recently as fascism and communism. An anti-British and anti-American animus became a hallmark of the Middle Eastern version.

The Failure of Pan-Arabic Nationalism and Ba'thism

The greatest harm done by secular Arab nationalism is the debilitation it has brought about in the countries on which it preyed. Pan-Arabism has allowed feudal Levantine rulers to escalate their quarrels by greater magnitudes than ever before, while enlisting the aid of oil revenues and outsiders to overcome the natural restrictions imposed by the size or wealth of individual communities.

In the Middle East, tyrants justify their repressive efforts by appealing to the higher goal of forging a pan-Arabist, racially unified superstate, and to the need to mobilize against the enemies of such lofty ideals. The bloody revolution goes on even after victory; internal terror and social devastation become synonymous with patriotism. This was true of the French and the Russian revolutions as well—models, unfortunately, for much of Arab politics. The archetypal despot Robespierre ringingly voiced the philosophy of regimes of terror:

> We must crush both the interior and exterior enemies of the Republic, or perish with her. And in this situation, the first maxim of your policy should be to conduct the people by reason and the enemies of the people by terror. . . . The spring of popular government in rebellion is at once both virtue and terror; virtue without which terror is fatal! Terror, without which virtue is powerless. Terror is nothing else than justice. . . . The government of a revolution is the despotism of liberty against tyranny.[29]

Elementally, terror and destruction are equated with patriotism. In a later speech, Robespierre noted that the difference between despicable despotism and glorious terror is not one of means, but of purpose. He also articulated another theme that has plagued European and Middle Eastern politics: the bizarre advocacy of gratuitous suicide.[30] Chillingly presaging Dostoevsky's fictional character Kirilov, Robespierre inspirationally applauded the nobility of a quest for death. The following excerpt from his last speech became the credo of the modern revolutionary mentality:

> Death is not eternal sleep! Citizens, erase from the tomb the inscription put there by sacrilegious hands, which casts a pall over the face of nature. Engrave rather this upon it: Death is the beginning of immortality.[31]

The worshipful pursuit of terror and of death serves two purposes. First, it disguises the inevitable failure of radical schemes by numbing the population into pliability and silence. Second, it provides vehicles to legitimize the excesses of ambitious rulers with absolute power, including attacks on any form of privacy. It allows rulers to twist the concept of *enemy* to suit internal political objectives. For Robespierre, the enemy was a liberal movement and anyone who sought to preserve any institutions that were not under state authority. These were barriers to his absolute power and ambition, and he used the language of patriotism to sweep them aside. Even Thomas Paine, the American pamphleteer of liberty, almost lost his head to the French Reign of Terror.

Robespierre's spirit haunts the politics of the Arab world. Pan-Arabic ideology is exploited by tribes, sects, clans, and ethnic factions to crush opposing factions, and by corrupt leaders who prey upon society. When local feuds are redefined in loftier, ideological terms—pan-Arabic versus antiprogressive—the violence and oppression are raised to new heights. And the embrace of terror and death follows.

With the empowerment of radical revolutionaries, the militarization of society, the centralization of power, and a windfall of wealth from oil, the Middle East became vulnerable to predatory governments at war with their own people. The annihilation of the cities of Hama (1983) and Chalabja (1988) by Hafez Assad and Saddam Hussein, respectively, exemplifies the mass murder that ensued. For more than thirty years, Syria and Iraq have been wracked by such governmental violence. Both countries' leaders have engaged in massive statist repression to eradicate all loyalties other than loyalty to themselves.

The Arab world is predominantly Sunni; but since Sunnis constitute only a minority in Iraq, Saddam dons the virtuous cloak of pan-Arabism to justify Sunni dominance in Baghdad and establish Iraq's "Arab legitimacy." Despite the ideological pretense, though, Shi'ites and Kurds recognize such pan-Arabism as a mask for Sunni tyranny. Maintaining and legitimizing this tyranny requires the Ba'thist regime to engage in aggression.[32] The Shi'ites and Kurds were the primary targets of the state's war against its own people—against Shi'ites because they are not Sunnis, against Kurds because they are not Arabs.

As the Ba'thist state apparatus has degenerated into a partisan instrument of annihilation, it has launched the region's two most intense rampages conducted by governments against their own people, both of them employing poison gas. The Syrian and Iraqi governments have killed more of their own citizens than have been killed in international wars in the region, and nearly ten times as many as have been killed in the entire Arab-Israeli conflict.

The Middle East has absorbed the deadly politics of modernity that led to Stalin and Hitler. This century's events have taught us that radical efforts to transform man and his deeply held identity invariably mean gulags and mass murder. The totalitarian state always descends into war on its own people.

Tyranny and Internal Instability

Violence also fails to achieve the one good that the West insists on, for which we are willing to tolerate repressive excesses: that is, stability. Even with its brutality, a tyrannic government cannot establish a solid, homogeneous nation. Not only does internal repression fail to change man, as most people do not easily forget who they are but rather maintain their identity persistently, below the surface; repression also unravels the skein of society, producing cynicism, thuggishness, and mafia-style social politics.

As the Soviet Union's collapse and subsequent fragmentation demonstrate, tyranny cannot surmount the "nationalities question"— the problem of competing loyalties. Rather than uniting people, repressive regimes accentuate their divisions. In a world of interlocking and highly intrusive security services, the primordial divisions such as family, tribe, or village become the only safe form of political opposition. Only those bonds that predate the tyranny are sufficiently solid, deep, and tacit to withstand and overcome the suspicions inherent in such a state's atmosphere. Newer layers of social organization are too easily infiltrated. Tyranny offers no path to regional stability or national cohesion.[33] As a result, tribal, sectarian, ethnic, municipal, familial, and clan allegiance have become synonymous with resistance to Ba'thist tyranny.

Pan-Arabic nationalism and Ba'thism have impeded rather than advanced the inhabitants of Iraq and Syria in the forging of distinct national communities. An Iraqi scholar, Abbas Kelidar, explains:

> Iraq and Syria have continued to have as precarious an existence as when they were created. . . . Although their political structure has become powerful and all-embracing, it has remained as alien and artificial as the boundaries drawn to demarcate their international frontiers. . . . The primordial ties of kinship—tribal, religious, ethnic, and family bonds—have remained paramount. Often they take precedence over national identity and interest. . . . [But] the ruling establishment is reduced to warring factions. Under these conditions, the state is unable to ensure domestic political stability or prevent external interference and sedition. Its survival becomes a matter of speculation for its own people as well as its ambitiously irredentist neighbors. . . . In the Arab East . . . the threat of disintegration is inherent to the system itself.[34]

As a result, divisive tribal, ethnic, sectarian, and warlord forces seethe under the veneer of unity and stability carefully displayed by the Ba'thist regimes of Damascus and Baghdad. As one Syrian Ba'thist candidly noted,

> Classic Ba'thism addresses three distinct factional divisions in Syrian society: tribalism, sectarianism, and clanism. The army and Ba'thism have been seen as ways to level the field among all the factions and to offer a superseding identity. It was hoped that over generations, through "political education" and by achieving economic equality, this superseding identity would take root and erase the divisions and inequities. But in the 1980s, the Ba'thist Party realized—especially in the wake of the events in Hama and the immediate threat posed to the regime by the Muslim Brotherhood—that its hold on power was still retained primarily through military force.[35]

Ba'thist nations teeter between repression and the warlord-driven anarchy that can overturn it. Factionalism in Iraq and Syria is likely to erupt into violence during either the succession of power or a major regional conflict. When the repression is lifted, the legacy of Ba'thism will be nations that are in shambles, vulnerable to the designs of their neighbors.

Elsewhere in the Arab world, other pan-Arabic radical attempts to transform societies have left a legacy of mass murder, destruction, and broken societies as well. This is a tragedy not only for Iraqis and Syrians, but also for Libyans, Algerians, and Palestinians. Rather than unifying societies, tyranny galvanizes primordial divisiveness. As U.S. policy on Iraq has shown, it is a very ineffective means of achieving regional stability. A regime that wages war on its own unarmed citizens is hardly likely to respect the rule of international law. Governments as internally violent as the Ba'thist ones cannot be expected to bolster peace or regional stability.

Tyranny and External Aggression

Assumption: Iraq's external aggressiveness—toward both its neighbors and the United States—reflects the nature of Saddam rather than of Ba'thism.

The grim prospects of eventual collapse in either Syria or Iraq, tragic as they are for their inhabitants, are not the immediate concern of others in the region or in the United States. Our more immediate concern is the politics of aggression that Ba'thist regimes are driven to employ in their attempt to survive. There is a causal link between the internal predaciousness and failure of Ba'thist nations and their aggressive, menacing bearing toward their neighbors.

A collapse in either Syria or Iraq would affect the other profoundly. Ideologically, a failure of Ba'thism in one implicitly indicts the regime of the other as well. Practically, cross-border tribal, ethnic, sectarian, familial, and clan alliances make it likely that events in Iraq would spread uncontrollably into Syria, and vice versa. Both Saddam and Assad recognize the intensely fractured nature of their nations' populaces, conducive to treachery and betrayal.[36]

Their very vulnerability has caused both despots constantly to seek hegemony over their neighbors. The Syrian and Iraqi regimes strive to avoid internal collapse by insulating themselves and by controlling external tribal politics and rival ideas. Effectively, they parallel their internal repression with external aggression, creating regional instability.

Ba'thism's proclivity for interfering with neighboring countries derives from more than tribal interweaving and porous borders—it is part of the movement's tyrannical nature. Pan-Arabic chauvinism and Ba'thism do not inspire the sort of patriotism that eventually forces regimes to accountability; pan-Arabic governments foment the external unrest necessary to make peaceful forms of nationalism impossible, so that they can dodge accountability.[37] They must be dynamic, perpetually pushing outward, or else they implode.

Thus the dark internal corruption of totalitarian repression is the source of external aggression. States that launch wars on their own people eventually escalate their conflicts beyond their borders. They must justify their repression in terms of a high moral purpose— as a putatively "patriotic" defense against fifth column supporters of the foreign enemy. Tyrants portray themselves as the agents and defenders of a noble cause, variously fascism, or communism, or pan-Arabism.

The lofty goal acquires the stature and authority of a new, secular religion that arrogates to the state the exclusive prerogative to define virtue of all sorts. There is no discussion of morality and patriotism other than through the state and its leader. Citizenship is defined not according to territory, but to loyalty to the government and its creed. Shrewdly, dissidents are redefined as traitors and heretics—dangers to the state. The line is thus blurred between the internal and the external enemy. Eliminating domestic factionalism, physically if necessary, can be justified as a precondition to confronting the ideological enemy. It is as patriotic and virtuous to kill a fellow citizen as to fight an invading army. Excesses and repression are not only permitted but are construed as duties performed in defense of this higher cause, in opposition to the relentless threat of imperialism.

For tyrants, having an enemy against which to define the struggle is indispensable. Abandoning the concept of *enemy* or embarking on an introverted policy would undermine the legitimizing structure of a tyrannical regime, by exposing the factional motivation of its repressiveness. An Arab nationalist state at war carries the glorious standard of pan-Arabism; at peace, it becomes no more than a petty dictatorship pursuing factional tyranny.

Tyranny and Anti-Americanism

The great nineteenth-century Swiss historian Jacob Burckhardt astutely discerned timeless political patterns in his study of the Italian Renaissance. Of the fifteenth-century princes, he observed,

> Nearly all of them were the result of recent usurpations. This was a fact which exercised as fatal an influence in their foreign as in their internal policy. The necessity of movement and aggrandizement is common to all illegitimate powers.[38]

Burckhardt's recognition of the inherent aggression of tyrants invites a reexamination of another key assumption guiding American regional policy: that anti-Americanism is a form of anti-imperialism, to be placated by deferential Western policies.[39] Anti-Americanism among pan-Arabic nationalists emerges from the same source as did Communist and Nazi anti-Americanism: the nature of tyrannical regimes. The hostility is a product of neither the U.S. presence nor its policies. Since the concept of *enemy* is essential to legitimize internal repression, neighbors or superpowers that represent ideas antithetical to tyranny are particularly threatening to the tyrant and are thus considered the most dangerous of its foes. In the Middle East, those enemies are the United States and Israel—not because of what they have done, but because of who they are, what they represent, and the fact of their existence. *External aggression, especially against Western nations, is inherent to all such radical, utopian movements, be they European or Arabic.* Anti-Americanism is the battle cry of tyranny, not a genuine call for liberation.

Since anti-Americanism is a direct consequence of the tyrannical nature of a government, any policy that appeases tyranny to pursue stability is doomed. The anti-American animus cannot ultimately be tamed by timid or toadying policies. On the contrary, such policies undermine the U.S. regional position by reinforcing the impression that tyrants can bring the superpower to heel through their superior will and ideas, thereby vindicating tyranny and its ideology.

For this reason, even if the *Wifaq* were successfully to launch a coup or to assassinate Saddam, we could expect the reemergence of a narrow Ba'thist clique controlling a highly centralized, intrusive, and tyrannical state rather than a decentralized, limited one. In fact, it is precisely the expectation of this result that makes the *Wifaq* so appealing to U.S. policy makers. But this is shortsighted policy indeed. A successful outcome for the *Wifaq* strategy would not change the basic contours, only the personalities, of the problem of Iraq and its antipathy toward the United States. What is more pernicious, such an outcome would leave the United States believing the problem had been solved. In supporting a coup, the United States promotes its own defeat and sabotages its resources for dealing with the ensuing upheaval. Even without Saddam, the prospect of another Ba'thist regime emerging in Baghdad should elicit our concern, not our enthusiasm.

Cutting a Hard Line on Ba'thism

Assumption: A real change in Iraq is possible only by encouraging a rift among elements of the narrow Sunni clique surrounding Saddam, including an offer of incentives. Broad internal pressure in Iraq against the currently powerful elite element reduces the chances of such change.

Will relieving some pressure on other elements in the regime drive a wedge between Saddam and the current Ba'thist elites, or will it cause them to rally? Specifically, does the existence of the northern safe haven and continued resistance from outside the Ba'thist, Sunni core of the regime encourage or retard the demise of Saddam's regime?

There is nearly a consensus within the American policy community that constructing a set of incentives—for example, the promise of forgiveness in the event of Saddam's overthrow, or of relief from some current external pressure, such as that created by northern Iraq—would encourage moderate Ba'thists, help them prevail within their system, and eventually embolden them to reform Ba'thism. In effect, such incentives would produce an Iraqi Gorbachev.[40]

But the goal is not to find an Iraqi Gorbachev who would serve as the agent for unraveling the Ba'thist system upon assuming power. The goal is to determine the measures we must use, to be imposed both from outside and from within Iraq, to compel any actual or potential Baghdad regime to jettison the destructive politics of totalitarianism. The debate over how to encourage Ba'thists to reform futilely reprises the debates of the 1980s on effecting change in the Soviet Union. The issue was not whether it would be nice to find a Communist to serve as the West's Trojan horse; rather, it was how to craft a set of incentives that would encourage Communists to be Trojan horses for the West.

During the cold war, some Westerners believed that incentives to the Soviet Union would encourage and assist "moderates" in the Soviet system, while harsh policies would foster "hard liners" and discredit the moderates. Such a view assumed that real change inside the Soviet Union could come only from within the Soviet ruling elite, and that externally manipulated motivations were necessary to nurture and vindicate the acceptable moderates. This policy collapsed at the end of the 1970s and early 1980s, as the Soviets exploited their engagement with their adversary, the West, to paralyze that adversary: they caused us to forget who we were and what it was we wanted. The Soviet Union then seized the strategic initiative and eventually waged war. Communist leaders, as tyrants seeking foremost to survive, understood that surrendering the goal of an eventual global revolution or neglecting to recognize an enemy serves to undermine the legitimacy of a government. When a nation's top leadership surrenders its informing ideas, then the will to patriotic sacrifice fades and repression is seen for what it is: corruption. Without the focus on the external enterprise, the government could no longer distract the people from passing judgment on itself. Communism, if forced to show a "human face" and come to terms with its limitations, faces implosion and eventually dies. It was unreasonable to expect Communists to embark voluntarily on a path to suicide. Shrewdly, Communists accepted the benevolence of the West while unswervingly prosecuting their war on us, exploiting our folly to vindicate the superiority of their ideas. To bury communism, Communists needed to lose that war and forcibly surrender their informing ideas.

Eventually communism was destroyed, and from outside the system. The external pressure forcibly denied communism the momentum and the opportunity for aggrandizement upon which it fed. Unrelenting military pressure from the United States (such as the strategic defense initiative program), hard-line arms control policies, and the insurgencies in Afghanistan and Nicaragua forced the regime to postpone indefinitely communism's long-promised victory. Combined political and military pressure discredited communism's intellectual foundations and eventually forced its collapse. Facing a resurgent West in the 1980s, even ardent Communists were left doubting, paralyzed, and vulnerable to the first credible push that would sweep them aside.

The robust Western challenge to communism also encouraged anti-Communist underground human rights movements in Eastern Europe, acting in concert with the West. Alone and beleaguered as people felt behind the iron curtain, still they were aware of the vibrant and powerful world outside the curtain that steadily besieged their Communist oppressors. This awareness emboldened them.

Together, the external pressure and the inspirited internal dissidents ineluctably proved the falsity of the Communist utopia and buttressed the resilience of the West. Radio Free Europe, human rights policies, and constant pressure on strategic issues were instrumental. Unrelenting pressure forced even Communists within the government to question their ability to survive, to attempt reforms to salvage the system, or to cut deals with the West. The Gorbachev phenomenon was the last, desperate effort of Russian Communists to withstand the West's inexorable assault on their system. The effort failed. In fact, it further undermined the Communist idea, which collapsed in 1991. Rather than salvage the system through broad-based reform, Gorbachev only accelerated its demise.

Pressure, not finely calibrated policies, encouraged many in the Soviet government to back off or to help bring down the system. Earlier efforts to help so-called moderates, along with policies designed to make the West and its ideas appear less "threatening" to the Soviet Union, were counterproductive and served only to prolong the cold war. These solicitous policies weakened the objective of exposing communism as a failed utopia. They tarnished the prestige of Western ideas, demoralized those trapped behind the iron curtain who were willing to make sacrifices, and stiffened the Communists' self-confidence. It was instead the policy of support for those who shared Western ideas, along with the revelation of communism as being intellectually and politically moribund, that finally succeeded in energizing the dissident community and solidifying its loyalty. This success had far-reaching significance, as the dissidents eventually assumed control in the wake of communism's collapse.

The experience of vanquishing communism can help inform current Iraq policy. The United States cannot lure Ba'thist leadership into suicide through a program of incentives, either by rewarding Ba'thist officers promising to launch coups or by abandoning the northern safe haven so as to ameliorate Ba'thist humiliation. The ruling elite will continue to view Saddam's repressiveness and his anti-Americanism as essential to their factional and personal survival. Even when Saddam ultimately falls, they can be expected to drift toward whatever anti-American movement rises regionally and globally. Ba'thism produces Saddam-like creatures; only their sophistication varies. All engagement with the West appears to the Ba'thists as a form of war to ensure their personal, factional, and ideological survival.

We must instead plan for Ba'thists to lose on an ideological as well as a personal level. Both Saddam *and* the regime's underlying ideas must be challenged and replaced. This defeat can be reinforced only by constant *and broad* pressure, both inside Iraq and internationally. As has been demonstrated by the democratic juggernaut in Eastern Europe, it is crucial that we support those outside the Iraqi system who seek revolutionary change—chiefly, the Iraqi National Congress—rather than place our hope for salvation naively on those within the system. The stronger the challenge from the West, the harder those inside and around Iraq will labor to subvert not only Saddam but Ba'thism itself. A resolute challenge instills confidence among Iraqis who wish to align with revolutionary change in Baghdad, and it raises self-doubts among those within the regime. Only by driving home the inevitability of the regime's defeat will we persuade its members to make their peace preemptively and defect, for the Ba'thist state "rides the tiger"—it constantly fears the retribution of those it tried to eradicate.

An open, aggressive, and relentlessly pressing policy is needed to undermine Ba'thism and its propaganda of omnipotence. Saddam's regime, the military, and the Ba'thist Party rely on that myth to avert mass defection to the Iraqi National Congress in northern Iraq. Indeed, if there *were* any dissident elements within the Ba'thist system, they too would be assisted by reinforcing a recognition of the utter failure of the Ba'thist regime. This failure is exposed by sustaining the pressure on Iraq and by humiliating and damaging Saddam's leadership whenever possible. Defending the safe haven and establishing a provisional government, rather than supporting a military coup, will enable the Iraqis within the regime and outside of it to revolt.

4

Iran, Shi'ism, and the Islamic Revolution

When the advocates of revolution in the Arab world seized power and implemented their attack on religion and on the traditional fabric of society, wherein family lineage is of supreme importance, they destroyed but they could not build. They left a devastated, pillaged, and intensely fractured social order in their wake. And having introduced to the region nihilist, utopian ideas, they redefined politics and set a precedent for other forms of revolutionary totalitarian movements.

The secular attempt to alter Arab society radically was soon challenged. The vacuum it created was filled by a renewed, zealous religious movement led by savagely ambitious men, which jolted and transformed Arab society yet again. Many of the leading lights of the religious fundamentalist movement began as secular pan-Arabic nationalists.[1] They eventually abandoned their pan-Arabic nationalist goals and crafted an Islamic movement that retained all the essential totalitarian and destructive features of the secular movement.

Secular and religious variants of totalitarian tyranny share a common aim: the destruction of all things old, traditional, and established. In secular, pan-Arabic nationalism, the state destroys traditional religion, along with every other potentially competing form of power and influence. The state then invents a new form of secular religion and social institutions, completely under its control—as exemplified by the popular festivals that originated during the French Revolution. The attempt to eradicate all social threats similarly exists in a religious totalitarian state, with the roles of religion and state being reversed: a radical form of religion seizes and reinvents the state, first obliterating and then reinventing all forms of civil society and traditional religion. Ayatollah Khomeini's Islamic revolt of 1979 was the Middle East's first, most important manifestation of this new challenge to both the traditional social elite and the West.

Iran and Fundamentalism

If Ba'thism in Iraq were eradicated, would its successor be preferable? Or would the overthrow of Saddam benefit the other dangerous power in the Persian Gulf, Iran, and its religious totalitarian ideology?

Wisely, the liberal philosophy of Western politics recognizes and allows for man's darker side—especially his proclivity toward ambition and arrogance. Niccolo Machiavelli notably articulated this insight during the Renaissance. The liberal revolution of the eighteenth century crafted governments to limit and balance the power of men over men, thus structurally ensuring humility. The will to good governance was committed to preserving the diffusion and decentralization of power.

The embrace of humility was further reinforced by religion, which presented an additional barrier to the state and to politicians: it designated areas of wisdom and power into which they could not tread. Reforming man's fundamentally flawed nature and creating a utopia, or heaven on earth, were deemed to be divine prerogatives that no mundane potentate dared to usurp. The American Revolution represents the practical application of such ideas.

By contrast, the French Revolution and the intellectual movement from which it sprang rejected the divine, instead celebrating the power and imagination of man to investigate and to control. This ethos respected no limits, and even human nature was fair game for the meddling of politicians. By appropriating the role of the divine, men could contemplate the perfection of mankind—and utopia was considered to be within man's reach. Proponents of the secular ideology assumed the prerogative to shape and reshape mankind according to their concept of perfection. Good government was defined as the concentration of power purposively focused on a utopian objective—an idea completely antithetical to the spirit of the American Revolution and eighteenth-century liberalism.

The Islamic revolution shares with secular ideologies much of what is repugnant and dangerous in them. Both religious and secular doctrines strive politically to reform mankind rather than reform government to serve humans as they are. And both systems are vulnerable to domination by ambitious and ruthless men.

Followers of modern religious ideologies have intruded the notion of divinity into the mundane world of politics. Usually this has sparked an upheaval in the internal politics of the religion itself. Spiritual leaders espousing such an ideology claim the authority to speak on behalf of God. They profess to have a unique relationship with the divine and an exclusive right to impose the divine will on earthly affairs.

Assuming the same shape and methods as those of its secular analogue, the radical Islamic movement first launched a totalitarian attack on its fellow Islamic yet still independent-minded comrades. Next it broadly targeted civil society—the ideas and established institutions that it could not hijack, suppress, or eliminate. Traditional institutions were accused of obstructing the realization of God's utopia. Both forms of ideology, secular and religious, reject the humility inherent to Western—and early Islamic—enlightened liberalism and religious thought.[2]

Having waded deeply into the muddy world of power and governance, Ayatollah Khomeini's religious ideology was destined to self-destruct. As politicians, his government officials were obliged to offer a utopia not only in the afterlife, but also here on earth. Thus, despite its spiritual veneer, Khomeini's revolution included significant elements of crude materialism—much like communism.[3]

Religious institutions across the Middle East have for centuries been part of the official government bureaucracy, poisoning vital bands of civil society. This phenomenon is especially pronounced in Sunni countries, where religious schools are state-funded and -run, and where the chief Sunni cleric, the mufti, is appointed and paid by the government. The Shi'ite revolution in Iran of 1979, as well as the Saudi Wahhabi state, are particularly menacing because they so thoroughly melt the distinctions between government and education, between the state and civil society, between politics and religion, and between political expediency and virtue.

The state is a dangerous agent of religion, which is one of the most important guarantors of freedom. The need to separate matters of virtue and spirit from the arrogance of power was recognized and explored during the transformation of Western thought three and a half centuries ago.[4] And Sir Edward Gibbon warned two hundred years ago of the danger posed by the blurring of such distinctions. He observed how pernicious it is for the public state to presume to define private virtue. The Roman emperor Valerian appointed an official censor, whose task it was to establish morals. These would necessarily be

> Inseparable from the Imperial dignity. . . . The feeble hands of a subject were unequal to the support of such an immense weight . . . of power. . . . A censor may maintain, he can never restore, the morals of the state. . . . In a period when . . . principles are annihilated, the censorial jurisdiction must either sink into empty pageantry or be converted into a partial instrument of vexatious oppression.[5]

Gibbon emphasized that the clergy could usefully apply their influence to assert the rights of mankind. Yet when the connection between the throne and the altar becomes so intimate that the banner of the church is seldom seen on the side of the people, then every barrier protecting society from its rulers can be leveled by the dictator's vast ambition, and every fence extirpated by the cruel hands of a ruling council. When the authority of a magistrate becomes so formidable, it degenerates into absolute despotism, claiming the citizen's body *and* soul—as in Khomeini's Iran.[6] Gibbon describes the deterioration of religious governance thus:

> The ambition of raising themselves or their friends to the honors and offices of the church was disguised by the laudable intention of devoting to the public benefit the power and consideration which, for that purpose only, it became their duty to solicit. In the exercise of their functions, they were frequently called upon to detect the errors of heresy or the arts of faction, to oppose the designs of perfidious brethren, to stigmatize their characters with deserved infamy, and to expel them from the bosom of a society. . . . [They] were taught to unite the wisdom of the serpent with the innocence of the dove; but as the former was refined, so the latter was insensibly corrupted by the habits of government. . . . They too frequently relapsed into all the turbulent passions of active life, which were tinctured with an ad-

ditional degree of bitterness and obstinacy from the infusion of spiritual zeal.[7]

Gibbon's depiction of Rome aptly characterizes the secular religion of the French Revolution and the Ba'thist revolution under Saddam, and religious totalitarianism under Khomeini's revolution. His caveat about unholy alliances between throne and altar continues to be relevant for contemporary secular and religious radical utopian movements. More important, Gibbon's proposed solution continues to be relevant: that the weight of the altar can effectively counterbalance that of the throne, thus protecting citizens' rights.

Secular versus Religious Totalitarians

Regrettably, many Western policy makers regard secular radical ideologues as inherently more benign and rational, and therefore reformable, than religious radical ideologues. This has led some to believe that secular pan-Arabic nationalism, especially a Ba'thist Iraq without Saddam, could be used as a bulwark against Islamic fundamentalism. The assumption, as we have seen, recommends pursuing a coup strategy in Iraq rather than a broad-based revolution.

But the notion of taming Ba'thism is a dream. First, despite their enmity, a secular totalitarian regime can cooperate tactically with a religious one if doing so serves their mutual, primary strategic goal— prosecuting the war against the West. The very nature of Western values establishes the Western world, and America in particular, as the focal target for tyrants' animosity. That animosity transcends their hatred of each other, because Western values profoundly threaten their rule. As a result, these tyrants will pragmatically set aside their own differences, deferring resolution or limiting confrontation so that they can instead confront the United States. Precedents in history, such as the Molotov-Ribbentrop agreements early in World War II, clearly show the folly of assuming that the traditional rivalries between dictators preempt their attention and protect their adversaries. Similarly, throughout the 1980s, the Iran-Iraq war *seemed* to protect the United States from the menace posed by either country. It didn't. Indeed, the most dangerous alliance to threaten the Western world was just such a wedding of religious and secular totalitarian ideologues: mikadoist Japan and Nazi Germany.[8] The United States must recognize this political phenomenon and avoid similar complacency today.

Second, the problem with both religious and secular totalitarian states is not their religiousness or secularism, but rather their commingling of arrogance with power. Both are states at war with their own people. The pursuit of a secular utopia is as irrational, mystical, and fanatical as the pursuit of a religious one. The nihilist, Marxist aspects are its dogma—closed to debate, reconsideration, or challenge. They include the cult of death and martyrdom, the glorification of revolution, the embrace of terror, the deification of the revolutionary elite through divine ordination, and intellectual or racial superiority over (and hatred of) the West. All spiritual authority is usurped by the state through the secular ideology; no other institution can have any say regarding virtue or morality. Whether the state usurps religion or religion seizes the state, the result is the same. For a tyrant to jettison any of these attributes would jeopardize his authority. And such states are inherently adversarial toward the West. Judeo-Greco-Christian culture, like that of early Islam, recognized the profound insight that the divine is perfect but man is not. Any political movement arrogant enough to confound these two worlds and attempt to create a utopia, whether based on secular or on religious hubris, will fail spectacularly and will destroy the society on which it preys. Secular Arab nationalism and Khomeini's Islamic ideology share the arrogance associated with all twentieth-century attempts to transform man. The source of revelation, be it divine inspiration or scientific knowledge, is irrelevant; either way, we cannot wield a regime based on one revelation to crush a regime based on another. Any radical program to fashion paradise here on earth by redesigning man through violent revolution is perilous, and it will necessarily degenerate into anti-Americanism.

Third, continued American belief in the utility of Ba'thism as a bulwark against Iran's Islamic revolution will eventually corrode our purposefulness in containing Iraq, in maintaining an anti-Saddam coalition, and in seeking Saddam's destruction. Such a belief leads many policy strategists to conclude that Saddam's continuation in power, albeit "boxed in," is the best of several bad alternatives. But this way of thinking is self-defeating. An obfuscation of moral purpose and an absence of clear strategic objectives on our part are leading to Saddam's steady rehabilitation. Eventually Saddam will reemerge as a great threat, returning the region to the critically jeopardous moment it faced in 1990.

Sadly, the legacy of the gulf war has been a near decade of squandered years—hard-purchased time that has gone unused. The current

U.S. retreat from Saddam, enabling him to harass UNSCOM without penalty, to redefine the UN mission, and to penetrate northern Iraq, suggests that the process of Saddam's rehabilitation and reemergence is well under way. Yet it is wrong to suggest, as is becoming increasingly fashionable, that Baghdad's terrible regime makes Teheran's look better.

Any attempt to use one totalitarian movement to impede or balance another must inevitably fail, because the two can be expected to cooperate and turn their hatred on the United States instead. It was this failure that led the United States into the gulf war in 1991. As important as it is to avoid the disaster of replacing Saddam with another Ba'thist military dictator, however, it is equally important to ensure that policy on Iraq damages rather than benefits the Islamic Republic of Iran. Bluntly put, the objective of Iraqi policy should be as much to bring down Khomeini's Iran as to bring down Saddam's Iraq.

Effecting a Dual Rollback of Iran and Iraq

Assumption: An uncontrolled, broad revolt will lead to a Shi'ite fundamentalist regime aligned with Iran.

Both Iran and Iraq, and the ideas upon which the two states are constructed, are serious threats to the United States. How can we vanquish one without helping the other? Similarly, how can we deal either with radical, secular, pan-Arabic nationalism or with fundamentalist pan-Islamism without allowing one to benefit from the other's defeat? U.S. policy makers have long presumed that the majority Shi'ite population of Iraq would serve as Iran's fifth column there; but would it?

An effective policy on Iraq offers the United States an opportunity to endanger and ultimately to triumph over Iran's Islamic revolution as well. First, any serious display of American determination will cause the resolve, prestige, and confidence of our regional enemies to wilt, just as it will bolster the prestige of those who choose to ally themselves with the West. Launching a policy and resolutely carrying it through until it razes Saddam's Ba'thism to the ground will send terrifying shock waves into Teheran. Obsessed with the politics of survival, most Middle Eastern regimes shun losers and embrace winners. The dynamics of the gulf war and the popularity of the United States in its wake demonstrate this axiom. Accordingly, any success in destroying one leader who built his career on anti-Americanism will promote pro-American coalitions in the region, unravel hostile coalitions, and profoundly frighten those states and factions that have thrived on anti-Americanism.

Yet a far greater concern remains. The ensuing chaos of any policy that generates upheaval in Iraq would offer the oppressed, majority Shi'ites of that country an opportunity to enhance their power and prestige. Fear that this would in turn enable Iran to extend its influence through its coreligionists has led Britain and the United States, along with our Middle Eastern allies, to regard a continued Sunni control of Iraq as the cornerstone for stability in the Levant.[9] Saudi Arabia in particular fears that any Shi'ite autonomy or control in Iraq will undermine its own precarious stability, because an emboldened Shi'ite populace in Iraq could spread its fervor into Saudi Arabia's predominantly Shi'ite northeastern provinces. The Saudi government also fears that this upheaval could spread to predominantly Shi'ite Bahrain, or to other gulf states with large Shi'ite minorities.

The American and British fears of antagonizing the Sunni base of Saddam's regime and our determination to ensure continued Sunni domination over Iraq have paralyzed past efforts to deal effectively with Saddam, persuading us to acquiesce in his repression of the Kurds and Shi'ites. This fear of antagonizing the Sunnis informs the consistently unsuccessful policy we have embraced since the gulf war—of seeking to promote a silver-bullet coup or palace plot run by Sunni Ba'thist defectors in the *Wifaq,* rather than a popular revolution led by a coalition provisional government under an umbrella organization such as the INC. The United States abandoned the revolution we had openly encouraged in 1991, precisely because it comprised Kurdish and Shi'ite elements. We have also stressed the importance of maintaining Iraq's territorial integrity as the highest priority, while permitting the erosion and eventual disappearance of the U.S.-guaranteed safe haven in northern Iraq. But approaching Iraqi politics with sympathy toward pan-Arabic nationalism and deference to the Sunni minority has already led the United States into one war—Desert Storm—and may lead it into another.[10]

The survival of Ba'thism in Iraq is integrally connected with the survival of the Khomeiniist Shi'ite revolution in Iran—even though the two nations hate each other. Ridding Iraq of Ba'thism can sabotage the Islamic revolution and its regional allies. But we will not defeat Ba'thism by assisting some feckless Iraqi-based underground movement such as the Mujaheddin al-Khalq, which is actually an arm of Saddam's regime. Iran must be severed from its Shi'ite foundations. And this can be accomplished by promoting an Iraqi Shi'ite challenge. Ba'thism in Iraq is a minority, Sunni tyranny over the Shi'ite majority. The survival of so repressive a tyranny over the Shi'ites, even without Saddam, leaves Iran by default as the arbiter of Shi'ite politics in the region. The Iraqi Shi'ites, if liberated from this tyranny, can be expected to present a challenge to Iran's influence and revolution.

Shi'ite Islam is plagued by fissures, none of which has been carefully examined, let alone exploited, by the opponents of Iran's Islamic republic. The Islamic revolution in Iran of 1979 destroyed secular and civil society in that country and profoundly assailed Western liberal thought there. It also empowered a brutal tyranny within Shi'ite Islam to impose a narrow dogma onto what had been a very rich and varied tradition. At the core of Iran's tyrannical revolution within a revolution was a very socialist concept: to place the state at the disposal of, and as the extension of, the revolutionary elite. That elite could then launch a perpetual war against its subjects, to transform Iranian society (and Shi'ite Islam) along utopian lines—Leninist techniques welded to a medieval soul.

The Rule of the Jurisprudent

Like all twentieth-century radical political agents, Iranian revolutionaries understood the pivotal role of the courts in institutionalizing their power. Thus at the revolution's core is a concept promoted by Ayatollah Khomeini, the *wilayat al-faqih*—the rule of the jurisprudent. This amounts to no more than a tyranny of the courts, which are run by lesser mullahs under guidance from a "council of divines" and a single revolutionary leader, the *faqih*, or jurisprudent. This divinely ordained leader is recognized as being above his fellow men—a demigod, he alone knows God's design. The same structure existed in communism: the people's courts, the Politburo, and the cult of the leader—a demigod by virtue of his intellect in discerning historical forces.

Although the concept of *wilayat al-faqih* appears obscure to Western eyes, it is the source of the revolution's power. It was the bulldozer with which Khomeini razed the barrier between the clerics and the politicians. In his first months in power he judiciously used the courts to eliminate all the clerics in Iran who were skeptical about his authority and to enforce his minority view of Shi'ite Islam as the new orthodoxy. Faced with the powerful encumbrance of a Shi'ite tradition of opposition to government, the religious totalitarian must immediately label all schism as heresy. When such ambitious utopian schemes as Khomeini's revolution inevitably encounter abysmal failure, they must increasingly adopt fraud and sophistry to defend their revelation—often by attributing, through impressively intricate explanations, all difficulties to an external enemy operating in concert with an internal heretic. Khomeini's divine revolution soon degenerated into accusations of alleged conspiracies in every event. It engaged in lies with every utterance.

This new orthodoxy is rickety, and it has failed to flourish beyond the domain of Khomeini's courts and henchmen. Iraqi Shi'ite leaders have traditionally focused on setting an example and learning, rather than dabbling in politics. The most prominent Iraqi clerics earlier in this century—Grand Ayatollah Muhsin Hakim and Ayatollah Kho'i, whose educational foundation, now based in London, supports an examination of Shi'ite learning within the framework of liberal ideas—rejected a political role for Muslim religious leaders and emphasized instead their exemplary role.

Unlike those in Khomeini's Iran, many Iraqi Shi'ite scholars of this century have encouraged the Arab world to study rather than to reject Western society. They have long been groping with the problems of reconciling political power with religion and Western with Shi'ite thought. The Society of Kufa University, established by Muhammad Makiyah, represented a major effort to launch an Iraqi intellectual renaissance anchored to both Western and Shi'ite philosophy. Predictably, this privately funded institution (supported by Iraqi businessmen) was unpalatable to Saddam's Ba'thist ethos and his totalitarian claim to all aspects of Iraqi life. So in his first act of power in 1968 he destroyed it.[11]

The concept of *wilayat al-faqih* is rejected by most Shi'ite clerics outside Iran (and probably by many of those within Iran, too), taking their cue from the most revered Iraqi spiritual leader of the nineteenth century, Ayatollah Murtada Ansari. The current leading ayatollah of Iraq, Ayatollah Sayyid 'Ali Sistani, has reaffirmed Ansari's ruling, much to the chagrin of the Iranian government. Traditionally, Iraqi Shi'ite ayatollahs have jealously guarded the spiritual realm (*din*), which was theirs, from the contaminating influence of the material and mundane world (*dunya*), which was left to the politicians. In the words of Fouad Ajami:

An older clerical and scholarly tradition held that faith should be kept apart from grubby political struggle lest it be contaminated. . . . The sixth Imam, Jafar as-Sadiq, gave Shi-ism its scholarship, and assured its continuity, by stripping the notion of the Imamate of the expectation that an Imam should rule.[12]

One of Lebanon's most outstanding contemporary Shi'ite jurists, Muhammad Maghniyya, also supported this older tradition by criticizing Khomeini and his revolution directly. Based on Shi'ite orthodoxy, Maghniyya wrote a scathing attack on Khomeini that echoes the writings of Niccolo Machiavelli, Alexander Hamilton, and Sir Edward Gibbon. He argued that all mortals are fallible and given to vice, and thus even the *faqih* is "vulnerable to oblivion, to pride and vanity, to personal predilections." A Shi'ite cleric, according to Maghniyya, may serve as a source of emulation and instruction—a *marjah;* but he may not use religion as a basis for an infallible and divine claim to rule.[13] Precisely because of the moral imperfection of man, Maghniyyah distrusted any form of absolute rule that was rationalized by a moral purpose.

Shi'ism's Western Affinity

It is important to note that despite their presumed antipathy toward the West, the Iraqi Shi'ites were historically among Britain's most vigorous supporters. In the early 1920s a significant population of Persian Shi'ites residing in Iraq was expelled to Persia, after which Shi'ite politics in Iraq tilted drastically: in 1923 the Shi'ites began petitioning the British to resume full, direct control of Iraq. The leading Shi'ite politicians well understood the utility of the British in helping them to combat their growing exclusion from power at the hands of the Sunnis. Shi'ite *mujtahids* (scholars) and men of religious learning also agitated for British return.

Throughout the 1920s the Shi'ites sided with Britain and against the Iraqi government whenever a disagreement arose between the two, such as in the policy for military conscription. The Shi'ite efforts to restore British control over Iraq climaxed in 1927, during the annual 'Ashura commemoration.[14] Iraqi soldiers and Shi'ites clashed at the ceremonial observances, apparently at the instigation of Iraq's Sunni premier.[15] In the investigation that ensued, the Shi'ites appealed desperately to the British to assume direct control. This long-established spirit of cooperation with the British and the West greatly concerned the anti-Western, pan-Arabic nationalists, who conspired and then successfully attained control of Iraq; hence Saddam Hussein's rapid move to oppress the Shi'ites upon seizing power.

Politically, the Iraqi Shi'ites have traditionally been quiescent. This is not because their religious devotion was insufficiently powerful to incite them to action, but because the sort of spiritual faith characteristic of these Muslims is seldom compatible with zealotry. Even in their docile faith, however, the Shi'ites have fulfilled a vital function in Iraqi society. Their schools, called *madrasas*, have traditionally operated as financially independent institutions—separate from, and frequently a barrier to, the authority of the potentate throughout most of the past two hundred years.[16] These schools were financially independent because they were located in the holiest cities of Shi'ite Islam— the shrine cities of Karbala, Kadhimaym, Najaf, and Samarra—and thus attracted donations from devout Shi'ites throughout the Muslim world. Especially important were the immigrant *mujtahids* and the donations to sustain them coming from India, following the rise of the Shi'ite state of Awadh (Oudh) there in 1722.

The immigration of the Awadhi elite to the shrine cities in 1860 provided an additionally powerful boost, since these people bolstered the population of the educational institutions.[17] Being private, the *madrasas* were culturally, socially, and even politically independent of the government's control. In stark contrast with those of the local Persian Shi'ites, however, the *madrasas* under the Hashemite monarchy of Iraq conscientiously displayed their loyalty to the king, even during the most holy ceremonies and rites.[18] One of the shrine cities, Najaf, was so vibrant (and demographically Arab, rather than Persian) that it acquired semi-autonomous status and became renowned by both Shi'ite and Western writers as the "heart of the world," a "world within a city," and the "receiver of all the news of the world."[19] In this capacity, the shrine cities and Shi'ite institutions were powerful bases for civil society and for a tradition of political decentralization in Iraq.

This financial independence and relative autonomy is unique and has had a profound effect on the character of Iraqi Shi'ism. First, it anchored the survival of Iraqi Shi'ite Islam in scholarship, in which it was allowed to engage, rather than in political power, from which it was barred. Second and more important, Shi'ite schools in Sunni, Ottoman Iraq served to diffuse, rather than to extend or legitimize, the power of the state. This is true also of the leaders of the Iraqi Shi'ite community, chosen by their peers for the purpose of emulation rather than official political leadership. In fact, Shi'ite Islam in the Arab Levant has served as an alternative force to that of the state. Shi'ite schools in Shi'ite Iran also traditionally played a challenging or balancing role against the power of the government, although the Khomeiniist revolution broke this tradition. In contrast, Sunni schools in the Sunni-run Ottoman empire were extensions of state power, and they merely enforced politically useful versions of religion as orthodoxy.

With totalitarian Ba'thism's subjugation of the Iraqi Shi'ite centers—islands obstructing the otherwise totally engulfing ocean of the Sunni despot's power—not just Iraq but the entire Arab and Islamic worlds have lost one of their most important models of civil society. These independent institutions could have served much as Protestantism did in the Anglo-Saxon world, as a levee against the inundating absolutism of the state and as a foundation of liberalism and civil society.

Ba'thism in Iraq and the Iranian revolution have joined forces to turn the Shi'ite world upside down. With no clerical freedom in Iraq—in fact, with a war of obliteration being waged against the Iraqi Shi'ites—no Shi'ite entity has the freedom to challenge the narrow, controversial, and revolutionary form of Shi'ite politics practiced by Ayatollah Khomeini. Through their efforts to annihilate the fabric and the power of the Iraqi Shi'ite community, Ba'thists led by Saddam have effectively consolidated the religious legitimacy and supremacy of the Iranian revolution over Shi'ite affairs across the Levant. To dominate Shi'ism in Iran Khomeini had to decimate his opposition, but to accomplish the same goal in Iraq he was obliged to make no effort at all—Saddam completed the task for him.

Ba'thism's demise could potentially trigger a reversal of this misfortune. Liberating the Shi'ite centers in Najaf and Karbala, with their clerics who reject the *wilayat al-faqih*, could allow Iraqi Shi'ites to challenge and perhaps fatally derail the Iranian revolution. Comparably, in the Soviet Union, communism was undermined when the people's courts, the Politburo, and the cult of personality were abolished; without these weapons, power can again be diffused, civil society reestablished, the throne and the altar separated, and utopian movements at war with their societies disarmed. The reversion to an anti-*wilayat al-faqih* tradition would further intellectually besiege what is already a limping revolution in Teheran. For the first time in a half century, Iraq has the chance to replace Iran as the center of Shi'ite thought, thus resuming its historical place, with its tradition of clerical quiescence and of challenge to Sunni absolutism.

Unleashing Shi'ism in Iraq would threaten Iran's Islamic revolution more than it would threaten Saudi Arabia. Khomeini's use of the clergy was veiled despotism that has failed, and now it is vulnerable to intellectual challenge. It was for this reason that Iran abandoned the Iraqi Shi'ites to Saddam's wrath at the moment of their uprising in March 1991, withholding support in any capacity beyond token gestures. Iran did not want an intellectual challenge; the Shi'ites of Iraq are useful to that country only as opposition to Saddam. A free Iraqi Shi'ite community would be a nightmare to the theocratic Islamic Republic of Iran.

5

Past as Prologue—Iraq and the Hashemites

On March 19, 1998, King Hussein of Jordan met with Ahmad Chalabi of the Iraqi National Congress in Washington, D.C. The two agreed that they shared a common objective: to rid Iraq of Saddam and to do so with an insurgency crafted around the INC, rather than with a coup or with Ba'thist support. Together they prepared a letter that the Hashemite King Hussein presented to President Clinton the following day. It met with a rebuff. But the struggle over Iraq is a critical one in the century-long political upheaval in the Middle East. This is evidenced by the evolution of Jordan's policy toward Iraq, the current relationship between the Hashemites and Iraq's Shi'ites, King Hussein's embrace of the INC, and the king's rejection of the *Wifaq* and Ba'thism. King Hussein's choice of allies and acceptance of enemies suggest that the conflict has resumed between the traditional Arab elite and the revolutionary Arab nationalists—a contest that began during World War I, with the Arab revolt against Turkey. Let us examine the role Jordan is currently playing in Iraq and how that role dovetails with the INC's proposed plans for the post-Saddam era.

Jordan's Hashemite Initiative in Iraq

Jordan, which is ruled by Sunni Hashemites, can play a helpful role in ridding Iraq of Saddam and Ba'thism; in stabilizing the politics of that devastated country; in preventing revenge; and in lending a Sunni imprimatur to any initiative that involves a more broadly based opposition under the INC.

Jordan first moved against Saddam when Hussein Kamal, Saddam's son-in-law, defected to Jordan on August 8, 1995. Shortly after the defection, King Hussein began to remind those around him of his status as the deputy and heir to his cousin King Faisal II, the king of Iraq. King Hussein presented himself as the rightful leader of the Arab Federation that grouped the two countries in 1958, before the Hashemite monarchy was overthrown. A resurrection of that federation would constitute an alternative to Saddam that could be acceptable to all of Iraq's factions, sects, and groups.[1]

On August 23, 1995, King Hussein addressed his nation and the Iraqi people jointly—the speech was broadcast in Iraq. Although couched in symbolic language and filled with rhetorical flourishes and historical references, the meaning of the speech was clear even to Western ears. The king had launched an attack on Saddam Hussein's regime in Iraq.

King Hussein opened the speech powerfully by tying Iraq's Hashemite connection to its historic glory—as the source of the Abbasid caliphate, the origin of Shi'ite Islam, and the leader of the Great Arab Revolt against the Ottomans:

> Iraq, its people and soldiers have a special status in the hearts of Jordanians. This status is characterized by sincere brotherhood with which we lived throughout the long march, and which was nourished by the pages of shining history, since al-Humaymah [a village in southern Jordan], from which the Abbasid call began, to the time of the Great Arab Revolt [against the Turks between 1916 and 1920], which was carried out for the sake of freedom, unity, integration, and progress. This was the time when the revolt's army waged immortal battles, and from which our Arab army and its brother, the Iraqi army, came. Both armies were engaged together in immortal pan-Arab battles of our nations, and its martyrs and our martyrs fell cloaked with freedom and glory, watering our land and the Arab land with their pure blood.[2]

King Hussein reminded his listeners of the origins of Shi'ite Islam with the murders of the prophet Muhammad's son-in-law 'Ali and of

'Ali's son Hussein in Karbala, Iraq. The king then alluded to the modern era's notorious martyrdom—the murder of King Faisal II in 1958:

> As for us [the Hashemites], the tombs of our martyrs are studding the land of Iraq . . . . This has been our history since the days of 'Ali bin Abi-Talib [the prophet's cousin and son-in-law], his ['Ali's] sons [and Muhammad's grandsons], Hassan and Hussein . . . and finally in the era of Faisal II and his family, whose precious blood flowed in Karbala.[3] [Author's note: In point of fact, Faisal II was murdered in Baghdad.]

It is important to remember that the Hashemite family claims descent from the Prophet Muhammad. The juxtaposition of references to the murder of Hussein, a grandson of the prophet and an ancestor of the Hashemites, and to the 1958 murder of the Hashemite Iraqi king Faisal II, a cousin of King Hussein's, draws a connection between the two. King Faisal II was the son of the founder of modern Iraq. The martyrdom of Hussein was the event from which sprang Shi'atu 'Ali—that is, Shi'ism—some 1,300 years ago. King Hussein's allusions to these chronologically disparate events and characters reminded Iraqis that the Hashemite presence in Iraq predates the Shi'ite-Sunni schism. The rhetorical strategy meaningfully hinted that Jordanian efforts could serve as the salvation not only of the Sunni elite in Iraq but of the Shi'ite majority as well.

Then King Hussein proceeded verbally to link the stability and territorial integrity of Iraq with its Hashemite administration:

> We have left the fraternal Iraqi people to choose their own way and live their own life, and we hoped that the Sunnis, Shi'ites, Arabs, Kurds, and all the elements of its national fabric which the Hashemites had held together, would not be torn apart.[4]

He discussed the revolution of 1958, which ended the Hashemite rule in Iraq and which he said ushered in the period of "Iraq's darkest days." He observed that the rise of revolutionary, secular, pan-Arabic nationalism was responsible for unraveling the carefully maintained fabric of Iraqi society. Finally, King Hussein elliptically accused secular Arab nationalism of being the tool of foreign conspiracies— thus effectively challenging its legitimate Arab or Muslim credentials:

I have no ambitions other than to soon see Iraq emerge from the total darkness and its long night of suffering to see the dawn of its freedom and liberation from all the causes of suffering, be they internal or external. . . . I was [Faisal II's] deputy and heir to the Presidency of the Arab Union that brought the two countries together. He departed at an early age and was a victim of the conspiracies of hostile forces in and outside the Arab homeland. [5]

King Hussein ended his speech by reasserting the Hashemites' claim to being the true heirs to the Great Arab Revolt—which, he repeatedly stipulated, had been co-opted by the secular, pan-Arabic revolutionaries cooperating with foreign forces:

The Jordanians are the heirs to a Revolt, callers for awakening, always choosing the path of God and the truth no matter how arduous the path.[6]

This speech, filled with assertions and implications, reminded Iraqis and others of the central Hashemite role in the Levant. It also announced the formation of a new strategic concept for Jordan's future—a Hashemite confederation across the northern Levant that would end the Ba'thist regime of Iraq, isolate Syria, undermine Iran, and challenge the PLO.

But the speech did even more: it was a call to arms in a three-generation-long struggle. King Hussein, beleaguered survivor of the elite Arab establishment and guardian of its traditions, had declared war on pan-Arabic nationalism—the vanguard, since the early 1920s, of the revolutionary challenge to that elite.

In the months that followed that August 1995 speech, King Hussein spoke frequently on the destructive role that pan-Arabic nationalism had played in Iraq. He warned that the ultimate effect of Iraq's repressive system would be national fragmentation:

Iraq is threatened . . . I repeatedly spoke of the need to reach a national reconciliation among the three main elements in Iraq that will eliminate existing fears among them. Pluralism must be respected. . . . If this tribulation lasts, it must lead, God forbid, to a dismemberment of Iraq and to its ceasing to exist in the form we know.[7]

King Hussein also remarked on the cult of personality and the tyranny that had devastated Iraq, and he presented an alternative to the "collectivist" identity that has been so central to pan-Arabic nationalism since the time of Sati al-Husri. Michel 'Aflaq, the pioneer leader of Ba'thism, wrote that "to be an Arab nationalist is not to be an individual, but rather the limb of an Arab collectivity."[8] Contrastingly, King Hussein told a gathering of journalists in September 1995:

> Prophet Muhammad and Islam ridded us of worshiping idols. For how long are we going to worship idols in this age? Enough tragedies for this nation. Everything we are speaking about is a right of man wherever he is in this Arab nation. . . . We have suffered as a result of the mistakes that were committed in this Arab nation. If the individual has no worth in this Arab nation, then there will be no future.[9]

As the autumn of 1995 progressed, King Hussein grew increasingly bolder in proposing the resurrection of a Hashemite role in Iraq as a means to reverse that destruction. Addressing a Chatham House audience in England in February 1996, the king observed,

> But when the conditions reach the conditions that they have reached in Iraq, in terms of the violation of all that is sacred to us all, it becomes our duty, all of us, to do whatever we can to bring about a change and to end the suffering of the people of Iraq. . . . I think that this is probably one of the reasons why Iraq was targeted even in 1958. It is history, it is the cultures that have come together to make Iraq what it was: the land of the two great rivers, the land of human resources, of sources of energy. It was denied the chance to progress and then to prosper in 1958, and since 1958, it has gone through a cycle of continued violence. . . . We need that country, we need it, we need their people. They have a right to live under different conditions from those which have prevailed that long.[10]

Again he connected the Hashemites' rule with maintaining the social fabric of Iraq—this time, specifically presenting himself as the agent of its reconstitution:

> As far as we are concerned, what can we do? I believe Iraqis have known us over the years, our family was once a unifying factor in that country. They know that we have no ob-

jectives other than to see that country stable within our region. So, we have the trust and confidence of many, the credibility with many. We are trying to utilize that to the best of our ability to implore Iraqis to come together to save their country.[11]

King Hussein emphasized that Iraq was already a pivotal strategic battleground, and that Jordan had little choice but to engage:

Iraq is surrounded by many countries and many of them may have more interest than we have in Iraq, and that is the danger, that is the fear, that Iraq could turn to become a battleground for those powerful neighbors of Iraq who seek to enhance their own positions.[12]

Elaborating on his phrase "conspiracies of all hostile forces in and outside the Arab homeland" and specifying whom he defined as his enemy, the king continued:

It was fairly obvious that at that time, we had the Cold War in the region. There were divides created in our region, within the Arab family, and the movement that brought about the change in Iraq was essentially the Ba'th party, which is Syria and Iraq at that time—supported by the then Soviet Union and by Egypt.[13]

By accusing the Ba'thists of being agents of foreign (namely Soviet) policy, King Hussein drew a parallel to the pan-Arabic nationalists led by Rashid al-Gaylani, against whom the embattled Hashemites of the 1940s were forced to fight. These precursors of the Ba'thists were also agents of a foreign power—Nazi Germany.

King Hussein's message was clear: Iraq has been destroyed by Ba'thism, with the assistance of Syria and the Soviet Union. The king has advanced a claim to resurrect the Hashemite confederation between Jordan and a post-Saddam Iraq, similar to the confederation suspended in 1958 after Hashemite King Faisal II of Iraq was deposed and murdered.

Political Decentralization

What sort of government does King Hussein envision for a post-Saddam Iraq? The answer can be found in what the Hashemites have traditionally sought, as the purpose of the Great Arab Revolt. In the nineteenth century, Ottoman Turkey introduced in its empire a series of reforms called the *Tanzimat*. Under the influence of Germany and France, the Ottomans undertook political centralization to "rationalize" governmental administration. The centralization process ushered in the modern era in the Ottoman Empire, triggered widespread upheaval across the Middle East, and created a crisis of identity among the empire's subjects. Fashionable European ideas, both good and bad, circulated widely in this dynamic environment.

In the early years of the twentieth century, Arabs revolted against the Turks, who were progressively appropriating all the newly centralized power. At first the rebels were not seeking Arab sovereignty—only some degree of local authority and autonomy within the framework of the Ottoman empire. The rebels, many of whom had traditionally wielded considerable local authority, meant to reverse the process of centralization that was corroding the empire and their power. The hopes of these Arabs were dashed by the Young Turks' revolt, which further centralized and "Turkified" the administration of the empire. Since the authorities refused to loosen their grip, those who sought greater autonomy had only one choice: secession.

The rebellion that was undertaken to change the empire's administration became a war of secession. The Great Arab Revolt, from which springs both the Hashemite and the pan-Arabic nationalist movements, was born of the quest for decentralization of power. It was a response to the crisis of identity kindled by the corrupt, unresponsive, intrusive, ethnically cliquish, and centralized Ottoman state.

Created by a coalitional effort with the traditonal Arab leadership to achieve administrative decentralization, pan-Arabic nationalism and its religious analogue, the pan-Islamic revolutionary movement, were shadows of the modern insanity gripping Europe in the twentieth century. In contrast with the Hashemite efforts, the pan-Arabic nationalists' pursuit of decentralization was akin to the early Communists' quest for anarchy in Russia. As part of the mission to seize power and establish a totalitarian structure, these movements first needed to undo the status quo authority. The call for anarchy and decentralization were tactical objectives—preludes to the eventual totalitarian and intensely centralized appropriation of power.

Pan-Arabism and pan-Islamism offered the angry and the young of a roiling Arab society a purpose that gripped their imagination: that of destruction, violence, and glory. These movements also offered the temptation of absolute power to the ambitious. But it was neither their Arab nor their Islamic objectives that came foremost: rather, it was their common totalitarianism. The Arab radical movements were infected by modernity's disease.

The Hashemite concept is quite different, and it represents a hope for the future. It envisages an evolution toward decentralized, loosely bound nations. Specifically, the Hashemites embrace the idea of a federated Iraqi entity, with maximum autonomy residing in local bases of power, broadly tied to a Jordanian-Iraqi confederation. In essence, this design harks back to the old Ottoman *Millet* system—decentralized administration along ethnic, sectarian, regional, and community lines—that was abandoned during the *Tanzimat* reforms.

The effort to pursue pan-Arabic integration, which failed in every other respect, did achieve its most damaging purpose: it undermined the regime's introverted or benign forms of nationalism. This was accomplished because the concentration of power in an intrusive centralized government, unmitigated by the existence of independent civil and public institutions, aggravated the normal competition among factions to the intensity level of wars of annihilation. Blood feuds turned into genocide, political disagreements into executions and gulags.

Much of the failure to deal effectively with Iraq can be attributed to the U.S. government's sympathy with the secular Arab nationalist elite, whose agenda to secure its factional interests was pursued at the expense of other factions—and of the effort to build a state. Many Sunnis, especially the Hashemites, closely ally themselves with the West's interests and demonstrate an understanding of the need to build states upon allegiance rather than submission. But the abuse of pan-Arabic regional solidarity by secular Arab nationalism, in Iraq and other areas, has been a catastrophically destructive element in the Middle East since the 1950s. This abuse is equally true of non-Sunnis, such as the 'Alawites in Syria, who used the concept of pan-Arabic racial solidarity to overcome their minority status. The politics of externalization and the dreams of utopia offer no salvation, only dire threat, for every regional minority. Their solution must be local, not universal.

Factionalism per se is not the problem bedeviling the Arab world, and it need not doom efforts to forge nations. Instead, its forces could be harnessed through voluntary associations, alliances, and unions—seeds of real, viable states. In fact, for much of the Arab world, factionalism constitutes the sole barrier against the absolute power of its tyrants. A more stable and safe society can be expected to emerge from the voluntary association of factions around a coordinating but diffuse governmental body. This was the case in the early 1920s, when the Hashemite King Faisal I of Iraq forged his nation by negotiating tribal alliances and unions. Iraq was founded upon, rather than opposed to, these primordial ties that define Arab society.

Despite the current grimness of prospect for a country trapped between totalitarian despotism and anarchy, hope is emerging for Iraq. The inhabitants of Syria and Iraq will persevere in defining themselves though their families, tribes, and clans. U.S. strategic policy in the Levant must be informed by a recognition of Ba'thism's deterioration and the perseverance of tribes and clans. Our policy should encourage voluntary alliances among these various factions—loyalty to which will serve as a barrier to state repression. These group identities contain the nuclei of nations. In the long and painstaking process of recreating civil society in Iraq, clan unions and limited governments alone can develop geographic entities into true states.

Jordan and the INC

Jordan's ally in the effort to restore decentralization and traditional politics to the area and wage war on pan-Arabic nationalism is the Iraqi National Congress. Ahmad Chalabi, its leader, has a long history with the Hashemite family, dating back to the earliest days of the modern Iraqi nation. Instrumental in designing the new country's educational structure, Ahmad Chalabi's grandfather 'Abd al-Hussein al-Chalabi served eight times as minister of education in Hashemite Iraq.

The elder Chalabi and his family were thrust into the forefront of the conflict with the emerging pan-Arabic nationalist movement led by Sati al-Husri, the intellectual founder of Ba'thism. While Chalabi was minister of education, Sati al-Husri was appointed between 1923 and 1927 as director general of education—eclipsing the real ministers, who were usually Shi'ite. Al-Husri was determined to centralize the educational structure under his authority, a vital precondition to effect the radical change he sought in Arab society. In contrast, the Shi'ites in general and Chalabi in particular wanted a decentralized educational system—with schools being run by local governments and ethnic, tribal, or sectarian communities. Al-Husri's views and power brought him into bitter conflict with Chalabi, whom he called the "clown of Iraqi governments," and with the Shi'ites, whom he dismissed as an "ignorant and backward" sect.[14] One scholar of the Iraqi

Shi'ites describes what lay at the heart of the al-Husri-Chalabi antipathy:

> The Shi'ites resented Husri, whom they perceived as an outsider in Iraq. They disliked his educational philosophy and his nationalist ideology, which ignored the strong tribal attributes of Iraqi society, and opposed his advocacy of allegiance to national over regional bonds.[15]

Al-Husri, in turn, tapped Sunni Arab resentment of the Iranian Shi'ites to launch an attack on Iraqi Shi'ites and Chalabi:

> While Iraq's rulers adopted pan-Arabism as their main nationalist ideology, they repeatedly questioned the loyalty and ethnic origin of the Shi'ites. Beginning with Husri, who may be regarded as the founder of pan-Arabism in Iraq, the proponents of this ideology emphasized the fame of the Arab empire and expressed a desire to restore its glory. Under the rubric of Shu'ubiyaa, they presented Shi'ism as a subversive heresy motivated primarily by Persian hatred for the Arabs.[16]

Moreover, while Chalabi advocated sending Iraqi students to Britain and the United States to study political science, al-Husri instead chose Germany under the Nazis—and always screened students first for loyalty to the pan-Arabic nationalist cause.

Since those days, pan-Arabic nationalists, and especially al-Husri's Ba'thist disciples, have equated the aspirations of Iraqi Shi'ites with fanaticism and a subversive Iranian campaign—a view that struck a sympathetic chord with U.S. policy makers following the Iranian revolution. It remains the prevailing U.S. view, as evidenced by our current preference for a Sunni-led coup and our rejection of a more broadly based Iraqi government with a powerful Shi'ite aspect.

Regrettably, the Hashemite monarchy of Iraq was too tolerant of Sati al-Husri and failed to see the danger he and his followers posed—a danger that exploded in 1941, with the pro-Nazi coup led by Rashid 'Ali al-Gaylani. After al-Gaylani's brief regime the coup was overturned and the Hashemites restored to power, but al-Husri's followers eventually defeated the Hashemites in the pan-Arabic nationalist revolution of 1958. Undoubtedly, al-Husri's ideologically charged educational system played a tremendous role in planting the seeds of that revolution. The Chalabis were forced to flee, both because of their tight alliance with the Hashemite rulers and because of their own mortal opposition to the pan-Arabic nationalists' radical attack on Arab civil society.

Some years later, the Chalabi-Hashemite alliance again became useful to the Hashemites. 'Abd al-Hussein al-Chalabi's grandson Ahmad, who founded the Iraqi National Congress in 1992, had striven for decades to wean the Hashemite family away from Saddam's grip. Not surprisingly, this effort encountered strong resistance from both Saddam and the PLO—the latter-day disciples of Sati al-Husri. Their machinations eventually brought about Chalabi's expulsion from and indictment in Jordan.

Beginning in the 1970s, Ahmad Chalabi sought to reduce the royal family's dependence on PLO-dominated financial institutions in Jordan and to terminate the nation's economic dependence on Iraqi trade. A PLO-run monopoly then controlled almost all of Jordan's finances, governmental and private, and the monarchy was beholden to it. This state of affairs left the PLO with the formidable power to destabilize and blackmail Jordan—even after Black September 1970, when the Jordanian army crushed the PLO's attempted seizure of the realm. Until he cracked that monopoly, King Hussein could hardly afford to embark on any policy that displeased either Saddam Hussein or the PLO, who could incite a civil war in Jordan.

To erode the potential for blackmail by these pan-Arabic nationalist movements, Chalabi established the Petra Bank of Jordan. The idea was to create an independent financial base to give the royal family independence from the PLO-run monopoly. At the same time, Chalabi worked in Jordan against Saddam's regime, trying to disentangle the intricate web of economic ties that bound the two countries and reduced Jordan to being an Iraqi dependency.

The PLO and Saddam Hussein reacted swiftly and effectively to destroy Chalabi's efforts. The PLO threatened to foment anti-Jordanian unrest among the Palestinians in Jordan and to use its influence among the high-ranking Palestinians who dominate Jordan's government. Similarly, the threat of belligerence from Iraq's economic and military might had a sobering effect on the Jordanian monarchy. Both forces directly challenged King Hussein over Chalabi—a Shi'ite in a wholly Sunni country. Lacking an independent base to fall back on for protection or support, Chalabi was sacrificed for political expediency. Precisely because the Petra Bank had prospered and threatened the PLO's monopoly over Jordan's finances, Chalabi was driven from Jordan. Once gone, he was indicted in absentia by the PLO-dominated legal system. The Petra Bank, which had flourished under his direction, was confiscated by his opponents and deliberately driven into bankruptcy within a year. Saddam and the PLO had won; King Hussein was taught that he lived by the PLO and Iraq's graces.

This circumstance changed in 1995. First, King Hussein signed a peace treaty with Israel, which he believed was designed to establish close Israeli-Jordanian strategic cooperation. He was primarily seeking to control the PLO's power. Second, following the unrest in Iraq in the spring and summer of 1995, the king perceived that the regime in Baghdad was flailing, and he recognized his opportunity to confront Saddam openly.

King Hussein embarked on a confrontational policy against Saddam in the hope that Israel would assist him with regard to his potentially disloyal Palestinian population. Understandably, the king then welcomed Ahmad Chalabi, a partner with whom he could engage in this double-edged fight. At first, contacts were discreet and carefully arranged. By 1996 meetings were more open and were clearly linked with Jordan's campaign to threaten the Iraqi regime from within Iraq— to supplement Jordan's efforts from within Jordan, using Iraqi exiles. Both Ahmad Chalabi and King Hussein saw the northern Iraqi safe haven as a springboard and node of opposition activity. Iraqi opposition sources even reported in early 1996 that Jordan was trying to "counter Syrian attempts to undermine its role in Iraq by establishing a 'Jordanian presence' in the Western-protected Kurdish enclave in northern Iraq."[17]

Attacking Saddam's Core

No opposition potentially threatens Saddam's regime more than would an alliance between the INC and Hashemite Jordan. A coordinated initiative between these two forces would possess assets and legitimacy unmatched by those of the other Iraqi neighbors—specifically, 'Alawite Syria and non-Arab, Shi'ite Iran. Apparently a Hashemite-INC coalition is the emergency Saddam Hussein most fears. As one Arab newspaper noted,

> Iraq's unity has splintered. The north is now tantamount to an independent state and the south is beyond central government control at night. . . . Social relations have broken down in the central region, and Saddam Hussein now fears

that the victorious Western countries could agree on restoring the monarchy. . . . Saddam Hussein's past suspicions regarding the Hashemite story in Iraq turned into convictions. . . . Because he has felt that memories of the Hashemite rule have been revived among the Iraqi public, Saddam has instructed his media to move promptly and to dig up the past in a manner that distorts the family's image in Iraq.[18]

Though a Sunni, King Hussein has solid credentials among the Shi'ites. They are impressed by his genealogical descent from Muhammad the Prophet and by the fact that his two early ancestors Ali and Hussein (from whom the movement of Shi'ism sprang), as well as his cousin King Faisal II of Iraq, were martyred in Iraq. The Shi'ites venerate the prophet and his lineage more than the Sunnis do.

As the legitimate inheritor of the Iraqi-Jordanian Hashemite confederation of 1958, King Hussein has remained closely tied to the elite of Iraqi society. Hence he has been able to undermine Saddam's support from many of the tribes upon whom the Iraqi dictator depends. Unlike Saddam, the king enjoys broad tribal, sectarian, and ethnic support in Iraq.

An alliance between King Hussein and the INC also necessarily contains a Kurdish element. The INC encompasses the entire Iraqi opposition spectrum, excepting those groups working with Syria's dictator, Assad. By coordinating with the INC, the king gives his Hashemite initiative an Iraqi face. Moreover, the INC's presence in northern Iraq gives Jordan a populated geographic base—northern Iraq—from which to operate. In turn, King Hussein's ties to the INC help to allay the fears harbored by many Iraqi Sunnis that the fall of Saddam and Ba'thism will be attended by Kurdish and Shi'ite revenge killings. A Sunni himself, King Hussein's imprimatur on an opposition effort is valuable.

King Hussein offers the INC a chance to exploit traditional Hashemite ties to Iraqi society, enabling the INC to infiltrate the tribal base surrounding Saddam. The INC benefits by having an Arab country as its mentor; King Hussein benefits by having an Iraqi faction as his ally.

Jordan against the Vanguard of Revolution

Jordan's 1995 initiative presented a great opportunity for the West and its key regional allies, Israel and Turkey. But pan-Arabic nationalist groups, which included not only Iraq but also the PLO, Syria, and Egypt, understood the threat that King Hussein's initiative posed. Consequently, they attacked his plan as soon as it was unveiled, piously warning that Jordan's policies would lead to the "breakup of Iraq." Consequently, in the fall of 1995 the Arab world braced for a cataclysmic eruption of the long dormant regional struggle to define the nature of Arab politics and identity.

What most differentiates the pan-Arabic nationalists from the traditional leadership is the attitude toward centralization: the nationalists emphasize centralized statism, the old guard, decentralized civil society. During the Great Arab Revolt against the Ottomans, decentralization was a strategy for survival for the Hashemites and the traditional, powerful families; contrastingly, the pan-Arabic nationalists initially used decentralization as a tactic to terminate Ottoman control, then proceeded to effect a radical reconcentration of power, to create a revolution in Arab society under a new elite. In modern times, the centralization of power has emerged as the foremost theme of the renewed conflict between the pan-Arabic nationalists and the Hashemites. Effectively, the words *decentralization, breakup, federalism,* and *confederalism* are coded references to the great struggle between the pan-Arabic, nationalist, revolutionary leadership on the one hand and the Hashemites and traditional leadership on the other. At issue are two fundamentally different ways of organizing Arab society and defining the Arab identity.

6

Common Cause—Jordan and
the Iraqi National Congress

King Hussein's move was risky; he chose to engage in a contest against formidable rivals who are all far more powerful than he. To win, the king required the close cooperation (if not protection) of America, Israel, and Turkey. He also needed to move quickly to exploit Saddam's weakness and to preempt his adversaries, who were also exploiting Saddam's weakness, as events rapidly transpired from March through September 1995. The longer the Iraq problem remained unresolved, the less likely it would be that King Hussein could succeed, or even survive, in this important initiative. After September 1995, Jordan's antagonists and Saddam Hussein could regroup and undermine Jordan. By default, time took the initiative from the king's hands, affording Syria, Iran, and Iraq the opportunity to infiltrate, plot, discredit, and isolate him. This is the current state of affairs; the longer it continues and the less support King Hussein receives from the West, the more endangered the Hashemites become. The Iraq issue could eventually bring down the dynasty.

The conflict with Iraq has become the key battleground in a regional struggle between two blocs. Iraq is the pivot; its eventual disposition and alignment will determine which of these blocs triumphs.

Jordan and the PLO

When King Hussein embarked on his war against secular Arab nationalism by staking a claim to Iraq and revealing a strategy to liberate it, one of his first concerns had to be the Palestine Liberation Organization—a pan-Arabic nemesis residing within his nation and to his west (the West Bank), colluding with the Iraqi Ba'thists. This collusion dates back to the beginning of the Hashemites' conflict with the secular, pan-Arabic nationalist challenge.

Uthman Kamal Haddad, the deputy head of the movement that was the precursor of the PLO, first brought together Palestinian nationalists who followed Jerusalem's mufti, Hajj Amin al-Husseini, with Iraqi nationalists in the 1930s, under the Nazi umbrella. Their aim was to strike down Britain, the Hashemites, and traditional Arab leadership. These common bonds and the purpose around which they were formed survive to this day. The link evolved into Arafat's connection with Saddam Hussein under the former Soviet umbrella. (The Russians are undermining the Hashemites presently as well, in a resurgent regional effort led by the former foreign minister, now prime minister, Yevgeny Primakov.)

In the war between the Hashemites and the pan-Arabic nationalists, the Palestinian national movement and the PLO have always played a central role. When King Hussein launched his initiative against Iraq in 1995, he understood that not only Saddam but also the PLO would challenge him. He knew this because of his experience a decade earlier, with the PLO's reaction to Ahmad Chalabi's creation of the Petra Bank. In the confrontation from which there could be neither retreat nor survival in defeat, King Hussein needed Israel's help to counter the combined might of the PLO within his borders and Iraq outside them. Specifically, he depended on Israel to assist him in challenging the PLO's monopolistic control of Palestinians on both banks of the Jordan River.

Managed by the prerevolutionary, traditional elite, Jordan has long recognized the advantages of tapping Israel's power, albeit discreetly. To some extent, Israel substituted as the champion that Jordan lost when Britain withdrew from the region. Thus Jordan turned to Israeli power for silent protection, while the PLO and Syria—for decades the vanguard of pan-Arabic nationalism, antagonists of Jordan and all it stood for—were significantly weakened by Israeli power.

Since the late 1960s, King Hussein has been threatened with overthrow by Yassir Arafat's PLO and with invasion by Hafez Assad's Ba'thist Syria. Jordan has traditionally recognized Israel as its ally in maintaining internal security by co-managing the Palestinian communities on both banks of the Jordan River and by extending a strategic umbrella against invasion from other regional powers. This was best demonstrated by the Black September uprising of 1970. Faced with an Arafat-led insurrection and Syria's intervention, King Hussein expelled the PLO and enlisted the Israeli air force to repel Syria.

But Israel's policies in the Israeli-Palestinian peace process have upset this tacitly effective relationship, thus compromising Jordan's position vis-à-vis the PLO and Syria. The Israelis have empowered the PLO in the West Bank and have offered territorial concessions to Syria. By striving to appease Arafat and Assad, the celebrated Oslo peace process has distorted Israel's policy such that the country paradoxically sides with the most treacherous, anti-Zionist forces in the region—at the expense of its natural ally, the Hashemites.

Perhaps the most damaging regional development of the Oslo process, coming at a time when Jordan relied on Israel to protect its vulnerable Palestinian "underbelly," was the controversial replacement of the mufti of Jerusalem. The late incumbent mufti—the Islamic religious leader who serves as official trustee of holy sites and heads the supreme religious council—died in 1994. A series of bitter exchanges racked Jordanian-Palestinian relations immediately after the signing of the Jordanian-Israeli peace treaty a few weeks later. Acrimony began when Jordan and the PLO each appointed its own mufti of Jerusalem to replace the deceased one. The contest had broad ramifications, since Israel's treaty with Jordan affirmed Jordan's traditional role as the guardian of Muslim holy shrines in Jerusalem. In response to Israel's concession to the Jordanians, Arafat lashed out, telling King Hussein that "he could drink sea water if he does not accept Jerusalem as the capital of a future Palestinian state."[1] The conflict over Jerusalem's mufti reflected the struggle between Jordan and the PLO to establish control over both East and West Bank Palestinians—pitting the Jordanian-Israeli peace treaty against the Oslo process.

Accordingly, the PLO officially called for a national strike and a day of mourning on October 26, 1994, to protest the signing of the Jordanian-Israeli peace treaty. Leaflets were distributed in the West Bank under the PLO banner, threatening King Hussein if he dared to enter Jerusalem.[2] The bitter standoff continued for days, with Jerusalem having, in effect, two muftis. Under pressure from Israel, Jordan relented—but not before King Hussein responded publicly to Arafat, ominously reminding him in a speech addressed to military officers of what happened to the PLO in the Black September uprising of 1970, and warning that he might repeat his punitive response.[3] For emphasis the king staged a meaningful gesture: he chose the granddaughter of a Jordanian soldier killed fighting the PLO in 1970 to present a bouquet of flowers to Israel's Prime Minister Itzhak Rabin. Thus he sealed the signing ceremony with a symbolic reference to the strategic cooperation Jordan sought with Israel against the PLO.

In coercing Jordan to accept the PLO's mufti, Ikrim as-Sabri, Israel demolished Jordan's influence over the West Bank religious establishment, which it had controlled since World War II. Israel was repeating the folly that Britain had committed in 1920, when it allowed a Palestinian nationalist mufti to be appointed in place of the traditional, pro-Hashemite candidate. The British had hoped that the appeasement gesture would pacify and harness the opposition, but it didn't. The mufti never softened his anti-British rhetoric, even after he had consolidated his control over the Palestinians; after his exile in 1939, he persevered in his anti-British agenda. And Israel purchased for itself and for Jordan the same trouble in 1994. As-Sabri continues to purge the Islamic institutions of pro-Jordanian notables, and he calls for both Israel's and America's destruction.

The PLO is methodically striving to debilitate Jordan. Children are taught in youth camps to sing about the day when Jordan (Karak) becomes totally obedient to the "angel of angels," Arafat.[4] The stronger the PLO grows among West Bank Palestinians by virtue of the Oslo peace process, the more influence Arafat gains among East Bank Palestinians—and the weaker King Hussein becomes. As the PLO insidiously creeps back into Jordan through the West Bank, Jordan haplessly drifts back toward the specter it faced in Black September 1970. To preempt Israel's shift toward the PLO, Jordan offered Israel a warm peace and a close strategic cooperation. But Jordan's offers and requested compensations were subtle; Arafat's threats and demands were blunt. Taking for granted peace with Jordan, Israel chose to appease Arafat, hopeful of averting violence.

The PLO and Iraq are also tangled together through the Arab-Israeli peace process. In the months preceding the gulf war, Baghdad originated the suggestion that the Palestinian issue fundamentally motivated its invasion of Kuwait. By the mid-1990s a mantra arose in the

United States, demanding that that issue be resolved so that we could cope effectively with the Iraq problem. U.S. acceptance of such causality and prioritizing in 1998—and the Clinton administration acknowledges this acceptance as policy—constitutes as much of a propaganda victory for Saddam as it would have done in 1991. And it erodes America's regional prestige.

Such prioritizing also serves Saddam's strategic interests. If he can influence Palestinian-Israeli relations through his PLO connections, then as long as the United States is willing to designate the peace process as a precondition to dealing with him, Saddam has leverage over U.S. policy toward him. The specter of this problem was raised on July 14, 1997, in Saddam's national day speech, when he openly called on the PLO to launch a war of attrition on Israel:

> The Palestinians led by President Yassir Arafat must turn this entity [the Palestinian Authority] into an opportunity to closely monitor and engage the Zionist entity and mobilize Palestinians . . . so all can bore into the Zionist body, weaken its power, expose its false and sinister claims, and exhaust it. . . . Arab diplomatic efforts must be devoted to supporting the Intifadah [uprising]. . . . The so-called self-rule area must be more of a base for revolutionary struggle. . . . Baghdad, as the symbol of the Arabs and Iraqis, shouldered what it shouldered for the sake of Palestine. They know also that the al-Hussein missiles were launched from Baghdad and Iraq—not from any other place—on the Zionist entity to declare, in the name of God and the nation, a position of defiance and Jihad.[5]

Saddam views his connection with the PLO and Arafat as a valuable strategic asset. Any U.S. policy that allocates a higher priority to the Arab-Israeli peace process than to the Iraqi challenge leaves the United States vulnerable to an Iraqi veto or sabotage, as long as the PLO responds to Saddam's direction.

Not only does the PLO maintain its strategic cooperation with and ideological affinity to the regime in Baghdad; it also publicly calls on Syria and Iran to join Iraq in forming a new strategic alliance to sabotage the tightening Turkish-Israeli-Jordanian bonds.[6] Moreover, the PLO has served Saddam by hiding proscribed Iraqi documents sought by UNSCOM in PLO offices and at its "embassy" in Arafat's presidential house in Baghdad.[7]

Saddam has further uses for Arafat in the warm PLO-Iraqi alliance. Saddam can again call on Arafat as he did during the Temple Mount riot of October 1990, when the PLO served as a strategic diversion to deflect attention from Iraqi actions and to complicate America's regional position. In fact, the PLO has *consistently* organized official, mass demonstrations in Palestinian areas on behalf of Saddam—as it has consistently announced official Palestinian Authority support for Saddam during PLO confrontations with the West.[8] It is also peculiarly coincidental that the Jerusalem archaeological tunnel riots of September 1996, which erupted on the PLO's orders, followed so closely on the heels of Saddam's invasion of northern Iraq, thus quickly refocusing the world's attention.

The PLO possesses veto power over the progress of the peace process, and the PLO maintains close ties with Iraq; therefore, Saddam possesses indirect veto power over the peace process. Any policy that makes regional strategy contingent on the peace process grants Saddam leverage over efforts to contain or remove him. Any U.S. policy that even remotely accepts linkage—let alone prioritizes the peace process as a precondition to dealing effectively with Saddam—offers him the ability to obfuscate our policy by eliciting resistance from the Palestinians. Perhaps the most significant regional threat posed by the PLO's growing power is the strength it provides to Saddam Hussein in the struggle between pan-Arabic nationalism and the traditional Arab elite—between Ba'thism and King Hussein.

Syria

King Hussein's stance signified almost as hostile a declaration on Syria as on Iraq. The Hashemites briefly controlled Syria just after World War I, until they were overthrown by colonial interventions, and their ambitions in Syria perpetuate that nation's enmity. The Syrian nationalist rivalry with the Hashemites has a particularly bitter history. One of the final actions of the preceding Hashemite Iraqi government (1921–1958) was an attempt to overthrow the pan-Arabic nationalist government in Damascus. In the 1950s, the former Hashemite Iraqi regent 'Abd al-Ilah (1939–1953) retained great influence over his protege, King Faisal II. Particularly in the final three years of King Faisal's rule, 'Abd al-Ilah redoubled his efforts to trigger a pro-Western coup in Damascus, to establish a Syrian-Jordanian-Iraqi Hashemite federation, and to install himself as the king of Syria. He was assisted in these unsuccessful enterprises by his rival Nuri as-Said, for politically complex reasons.[9]

The Hashemites themselves had good reason to fear the extraterritorial ambitions of pan-Arabic nationalists in Damascus. Sati al-Husri, the intellectual founder of modern Ba'thism and the mentor of Iraq's pan-Arabic nationalists, was deported from Baghdad to Syria when the Hashemites restored their rule and expelled the pro-Nazi government under Rashid al-Gaylani in May 1941.[10] Once in Syria, al-Husri established himself as a leading figure in the educational structure; he even wrote the national educational syllabus, upon which a new generation of radical pan-Arabic nationalists, particularly Ba'thists, were reared. Iraqi Hashemites understood that a movement was growing in Syria among those exiles whom the Hashemites had defeated in 1941. By the mid-1950s, that movement had seized power in Damascus.

Hashemite-Syrian relations have always been informed by these tensions. After 1958, the bitterness expressed itself in a Jordanian-Syrian hostility that included Syrian invasions of Jordan. In the words of one senior Jordanian official,

> I do not think that a day will come soon when the Syrians are free of their misgivings toward Jordan or when the Jordanians abandon their fears of Syrian ambitions. . . . We read daily reports showing that some senior party and state officials in Syria still regard Jordan as southern Syria. If we told you that we trust the Syrian leadership, we would be deceiving ourselves and you as well.[11]

King Hussein sparked a fierce renewal of this festering hostility when he launched his anti-Saddam initiative in late 1995. Within a day of Hussein Kamal's defection, Talal Salman, the editor of Lebanon's pro-Syrian *as-Safir* and a close friend of Assad's, wrote that "the scandal is in Saddam's house, but the danger is that the price will be paid by every house in Iraq and the neighboring countries. Could it be an American-Hashemite scandal? . . . King Hussein's Hashemite dynasty has an unfortunate claim to the defunct Iraqi throne."[12]

Syria's Vice President Khaddam was most explicit about the strategic importance for Syria of Iraq's eventual alignment, and about the mortal danger that King Hussein's efforts and politics posed to the Ba'thist Syrian regime:

[Khaddam] charged that plans were being hatched to break Iraq up into separate Sunni, Shi'ite, and Kurdish entities that would then be rejoined with Jordan in a federation that would be part of a new Israeli-led bloc in the region. He warned that such schemes would lead to the dismemberment of other Arab countries along ethnic or religious lines, part of the process of strengthening Israel's hand against the Arabs by fragmenting them.[13]

This warning is astoundingly candid. Khaddam was acknowledging that if the INC and Jordan were to prevail in their efforts to remove Saddam and to garner Israeli support, then the region's pan-Arabic nations, including Syria, would collapse. In defining the Jordanian threat in such a way, Khaddam approached an admission that Syrian Ba'thism had failed to craft a solid state. This stance contradicted the facade of unity so carefully cultivated by the Syrian Ba'thist regime. It revealed Syria's fragility and vulnerability; that its quest for regional domination was equally a quest for survival. An opportunity was also a mortal risk.

Khaddam observed, too, that Jordan's stance threatened not only the pan-Arabic nationalist but also the Islamic revolutionary effort. He told a Western journalist,

If such an axis [of Jordan, Israel, Turkey] were to come into existence, it would not be a threat to Syria alone. It would be against the entire Arab nation. . . . In addition, such an axis would also harm the Islamic states.[14]

Khaddam's warning was not empty rhetoric; Assad himself was shaken by Hussein's initiative. *Newsweek* reported that

Syrian President Hafez Assad sees the whole affair as part of an effort to isolate him. . . . Assad is so preoccupied that his aides have told visitors he is devoting himself full-time to the Iraqi question.[15]

Consequently, in late August 1995 Assad took personal charge of the Iraq dossier and formed a small-scale operations room under his control, with a team consisting of his most senior security, military, and political advisers.[16] In fact, so strong were his concerns that the Syrians bluntly told the Lebanese they had no time to allocate to the

Lebanese portfolio: "they cannot afford the fantasy of Lebanese problems now."[17] Lebanese government sources told Western journalists,

> Syria is alarmed by the prospect of a new government in
> Iraq. It fears being surrounded by a ring of pro-American
> states. . . . The Syrians say they are surrounded by the
> Americans in Jordan, Israel and Turkey, and now they fear
> in Iraq too. . . . The problem is really very serious for
> Syria.[18]

The Syrians were so rattled that they saw evidence of a Jordanian
plot around every corner. For example, when a pro-Syrian, Sunni fundamentalist leader and cleric, Sheikh Nizar Halabi, was gunned down
in Beirut by assassins in early September 1995, the Syrians believed
the hit was part of a Jordanian-Israeli scheme to destabilize their authority in Lebanon and to preoccupy their attention, while King Hussein pursued his ambitions in Baghdad.[19]

One of the first things Syria did to recover was to send Vice President Khaddam to Iran, to "prepare accurate plans to confront this new
and serious situation which threatens both countries"—plans that
addressed "the current changes in Iraq and the important role given
to Jordan."[20] In preparation for these meetings, which Iran's press
claimed were focused almost exclusively on the issue of Iraq, Syria's
President Assad sent a letter to the Iranian leadership calling for the
formation of a new regional bloc to include Syria, Egypt, Iran, and
Iraq.[21] Apparently Assad also asserted his desire to form such a bloc
during his summit meeting with Egypt's President Mubarak in early
September 1995.[22]

Syria and Iraq, both Ba'thist, both ruled by leaders with imperial
designs, may have been rivals for the claim to the pan-Arabic nationalist throne, but the menace posed by Jordan's maverick initiative
prompted them to suspend their antagonism and cooperate with one
another. As one Ba'thist expressed the plight,

> Syria may be locked in a historic and ideological dispute
> with the current Iraqi government, but it would rather deal
> with it than with the alternative regimes which the interna-
> tional media machine has begun to lionize.[23]

The leading Saudi newspaper, owned by a branch of the Saudi royal
family, commented,

President al-Assad seems profoundly convinced that it was necessary to unify the two flanks of the Ba'th party, the Iraqi flank and the Syrian flank, and consequently to unify the two neighboring countries. It was for this reason that he maintained his own channels . . . with senior Iraqi officials in the state, in the party, and probably also in the Iraqi armed forces.[24]

Syrian-Jordanian tensions escalated throughout the autumn of 1995, marked by a series of acrimonious exchanges between Damascus and Amman. Arab newspapers observed:

Damascus was quick to pick up the signals from Amman . . . about what kind of post-Saddam Iraq they envisage, and feels it is targeted by the prospect of a strong Jordanian role on Syria's eastern flank.[25]

In particular, Damascus openly accused King Hussein of planning a Jordanian-Israeli-Turkish strategic campaign to isolate Syria and destroy Ba'thism:

Damascus believes there are many indications [of a plan], including quasi-public Israeli positions supporting "far-reaching decentralization in Iraq," the expression used by Israeli diplomats to refer to partition of Iraq. . . . Damascus believes that Jordan plays a major role with regard to establishing a "natural axis" with central Iraq on one side and Israel on the other, which would isolate Syria from the Arabian peninsula and [in the words of the Syrian official] "squeeze it between this axis in the south and Turkey in the north. Damascus fears that this could be the prelude to a redrawing of the map of the Middle East along sectarian, religious, linguistic, and ethnic lines, which would threaten Syria's territorial integrity, something Assad could not accept."[26]

In October the discourse between Jordan and Syria became even more shrill. Syria's foreign minister, Farouq ash-Shar'a, issued a public threat in front of the United Nations General Assembly. As Arab journalists reported:

It is necessary to take seriously Shar'a's threat in his speech at the UN General Assembly that Syria would act to undermine the Israeli-Palestinian and Israeli-Jordanian agreements if they felt they were being used to "harm the national and pan-Arab interests."[27]

Jordan did not retreat. Following a series of particularly mordant attacks on the nation and its king in Syrian newspapers, Amman began to reciprocate in caustic, unguarded language. Jordan's foreign minister told one journalist,

> Syrian Vice President Khaddam has attacked Jordan more than once in the Syrian newspaper *Tishrin*, and in other newspapers and magazines. . . . Syria has been accusing Jordan of trying to divide Iraq. . . . I want to remind the Syrians: During the Gulf Crisis, who fought against Iraq?[28]

The answer to this rhetorical question, of course, is Syria.

In his most direct attack, Foreign Minister 'Abdel Karim al-Kabarati said at another forum:

> Jordan cannot be measured by its size or population, but by the role it [plays] and the mission it carries. . . . We do not accept being dictated to by anyone. . . . Would Damascus accept, for instance, that its role in Lebanon be considered interference in the internal affairs of a neighboring country—and by any standard, it is much bigger than our role in Iraq? . . . We will continue to play [our role], whether it pleases or angers others.[29]

Al-Kabariti opined elsewhere during that week that "there is a degree of hypocrisy and inconsistency in political discourse" in Syrian policy.[30] The acrid exchanges continued for months. In late November, al-Kabariti unceremoniously observed,

> It is obvious that Syria is looking for pretexts to justify its disputes with Jordan. . . . It has shifted to leveling charges in the direction of accusing Jordan of dividing Iraq. This is merely shifting from one pretext to another to maintain tensions and hostility toward Jordan. This is a form of political hypocrisy and duplicity.[31]

King Hussein entered the fray personally. On November 10 he said of Syria's Vice President Khaddam,

Such people were dishonorable and see only their own interest, believing in nothing but themselves, working only for themselves, and being too cowardly to shoulder their responsibilities.[32]

He also insinuated threats at the Ba'thist membership of Jordan's trade unions in his public speeches—threats clearly directed at Syria.[33] In response to these Jordanian counterattacks, Syria demanded a "public apology" from King Hussein.[34]

Not much was done to calm the waters in this conflict over survival. When Jordan's foreign minister tried to promote a détente by sending an emissary to request from his Syrian counterpart an invitation to Damascus for discussions, the Jordanian was coldly rebuffed by both the foreign ministry and Vice President Khaddam. The ministry announced that "Syria cannot at present invite any Jordanian official because it rejects all the political developments in Jordan."[35]

Not only did Syria attack Jordan; its officials also declared their own vision for Iraq and their demands on U.S. policy:

> Syria will demand of the United States Secretary of State sufficient guarantees to preserve a strong central government in Baghdad which can avert Iraq's partition and restore the authority of the central government in all areas— in other words, to safeguard Iraq as an entity with multiple religious, sectarian, and ethnic groups and with a strong central government.[36]

As it happened, Syria was preaching to the choir. By late 1995 the United States had already made the decision—for many of Syria's same reasons and preferences—to support the Ba'thist-run *Wifaq* coup group rather than the broad-based opposition under the INC. Although perhaps unwittingly, the United States was proceeding in parallel purpose to the Syrians and *at cross-purposes* to King Hussein of Jordan.

Then Syria, either unwittingly or in a deliberate move to press its initiative on the Iraq issue, manipulated the United States regarding the Arab-Israeli peace process. To preempt any potential pro-Western strategic realignment, Damascus reasserted its demands for a necessary linkage between the peace process and America's support for Syria's "regional concerns"—that is, Iraq. Syria's interest in the Arab-Israeli peace process is informed largely by that process's advancement of Assad's regional ambitions. Syria dangles (but never fulfills) the temptation of peace before Israel and the United States, in the hope of luring them into diminishing their support for Ahmad Chalabi and King Hussein.

In September 1995, for example, Assad refused to resume peace talks until his "regional" concerns—over Iraq—were addressed. On September 27, Syrian officials noted the linkage:

> In the words of a Syrian figure close to the negotiations with the Israelis, the talks were deadlocked not just over the [Golan Heights], but also because "we did not get convincing answers from the U.S. administration about the regional files. . . . There is no room for signing a peace agreement before defining Syria's position and role in the future regional map. Iraq's fate is the key to the post-peace game, and this is what Assad wants to discuss before signing a peace agreement.[37]

Syria's lure worked. In response, U.S. Assistant Secretary of State Robert Pelletreau hastened to assure the Syrians that the United States was not trying to use Iraq as a stick with which to beat Syria.[38] Afterward, American officials consistently issued public assurances to Damascus that America would not harm Syrian interests with our Iraq policy. Pelletreau stated in an interview:

> Washington's policy is not aimed at isolating or putting pressure on Damascus. . . . There was a lot of speculation that we and others might be trying to . . . put pressure on Syria through the policy we are following in Iraq, and I can tell you it is not true. In fact, we have had a certain dialogue with Syria about developments within Iraq.[39]

But Syria's problems are America's strategic opportunities. The United States should view an eventual realignment of Iraq with Jordan, Israel, and Turkey as a goal of supreme importance. We could reconfigure the strategic balance in the Levant by defeating the century-old supremacy of imported European totalitarianism in the form of pan-Arabic nationalism. Syria's alarm indicates just how close America, Jordan, Turkey, and Israel are to success, and how important it is not to allow the peace process to be used as a ruse to undermine that success. Unfortunately, current U.S. policy is determined to surrender this opportunity.

Lebanon's Regional Rollback of Shi'ite Fundamentalism

Syria has reason beyond the Hashemite-Ba'thist conflict to be concerned about Jordan's strategic initiative: a fundamental change of government in Iraq could undermine Syria's control over Lebanon as well. Furthermore, a shift of the Shi'ite center of gravity toward Iraq has larger, regional implications. Through intermarriage, history, and social relations, the Shi'ites of Lebanon have traditionally maintained close ties with the Shi'ites of Iraq. The Lebanese Shi'ite clerical establishment has customarily been politically quiescent, like the Iraqi Shi'ites.[40] The Lebanese looked to Najaf's clerics for spiritual models. But Saddam's destruction of the Shi'ite community in Iraq left Lebanon's Shi'ites adrift—prompting Iran to steer the community with ideas of its own. By default, Iran was able to assume the dominant intellectual role among Lebanon's Shi'ites, and its authority was reinforced by Syria's military might.

This arrangement was as beneficial to Syria as to Iran. The Shi'ite community lives on the front lines with Israel; its engagement is essential to keeping the conflict alive. Yet standard pan-Arabic appeals, which would justify Syria's occupation and absorption of Lebanon, were useless with the Shi'ites, who recognized such chauvinistic propaganda as a thinly disguised Sunni attempt to control Lebanon. To direct the Shi'ite community's thinking, Syria needed some ideology other than Arabic secular nationalism. Khomeini's Iran provided that ideology.

Historically, the Shi'ites of Lebanon have felt more threatened by their Sunni, pan-Arabist countrymen than by Israel. The massive influx of the PLO was calamitous for them. Not only did the PLO annihilate the Christian presence in the northern half of southern Lebanon; it also wreaked havoc on the traditionally unpoliticized and unarmed Shi'ites of the south. The PLO—radical, violent, Sunni, pan-Arabic, and secular nationalist—had been invited into Lebanon by Prime Minister Karami, a Sunni, pan-Arabic nationalist, precisely so that he could tip the demographic scales in a country where the Sunnis were a relatively small minority. Attacking Israel through Lebanese soil, the PLO converted the Shi'ite domains of the south into the main battleground of the Arab-Israeli conflict. The unarmed and vulnerable Shi'ites, trapped in the cross-fire, understood the true agenda of the conflict: combating Israel along the southern Lebanese frontier enabled the PLO to occupy and dominate the Shi'ite areas and convert them into Sunni strongholds.

Both the Christians and the Shi'ites grasped this strategy by the mid-1970s. When the Christians launched a civil war against the PLO in 1975, the Shi'ites were cornered: they had to organize and arm themselves or be annihilated. So the Shi'ites organized and armed, primarily against the PLO.

Sensing the threat from an emerging Shi'ite force in Lebanon, the PLO enlisted the aid of another leading figure in the totalitarian, pan-Arabic nationalist movement: Libyan leader Muammar Qhaddafi. In 1978 the PLO murdered the leading Lebanese Shi'ite cleric, Ayatollah Musa a-Sadr, who had been forming the Shi'ites of the south into a militia. Potentially, such a force would be capable of ejecting the PLO from southern Lebanon and liberating the Shi'ites from the cross-fire between PLO attacks and Israeli reprisals. Needing a point of geographic contact with Israel, Arafat seized control of vast areas of Lebanon—ostensibly to fight Zionism, but in reality to prey upon Lebanon's citizens and steal their wealth. Of course, he justified his mission in the name of "the struggle." Without his unceasing attacks on Israel, Arafat's presence in Lebanon would easily be exposed for what it was: a pillaging PLO, Sunni, pan-Arabic invasion of another Arab nation.

The politicization and arming of the Shi'ites was an internal Lebanese matter, undertaken to provide traditionally peaceful people with the power to resist the destruction of their community by the PLO. As mentioned above, Beirut's Sunni, pan-Arabic leadership had invited the similarly constituted PLO into Lebanon to help suppress the Lebanese Christians and Shi'ites. Hence the Shi'ites welcomed invading Israeli troops in 1982, in a direct repudiation of the PLO, Syria, and Iran; the Shi'ites had hardly built enough of a force to expel the PLO themselves. They also supported the May 17, 1983, peace agreement between Lebanon and Israel.[41] A majority (although it has since dwindled to a large minority) of the South Lebanese Army, the pro-Israeli militia helping Israel to protect its security zone, is Shi'ite—not Christian, as the press generally reports.

But Israel's withdrawal from most of southern Lebanon in 1985 opened the door for the immediate reentry of the Syrians, with a heavily Iranian presence. Only after this occurrence did many of Lebanon's Shi'ites became bitter opponents of Israel. They also became agents for abrogating the May 17 agreement, through the Hizballah—an organization, styled after Khomeini's Iranian Hezbollahis, that challenged the traditional Shi'ite leadership.[42] Still, the continued existence of the older, more indigenous Amal (Arabic for *hope*) faction, the growing tension between Amal and Hizballah, and the heavy presence of Shi'ites in the South Lebanese Army all testify to the strong residual resentment felt by the Shi'ites for the Iranian and Syrian domination of Lebanon.

The roles of the PLO (before 1982) and Syria (after 1984) in Lebanon have greatly damaged U.S. and Western strategic interests, effectively quelling the Lebanese Shi'ites as Saddam had done to the Iraqi ones. They crushed the indigenous, traditional, quiescent Shi'ite leadership, leaving a vacuum for Iran to fill. The PLO and Saddam intended to annihilate the Shi'ites; the ideological transformation they effected was an unintended result. For Syria, by contrast, ideology was part of the strategic plan. Following Israel's withdrawal from most of Lebanon in 1984, Syria used its alliance with Iran to dominate the Shi'ite community of Lebanon. The relationship between the Lebanese Shi'ites and Syria was always a fragile one; of Lebanon's communities, the Shi'ites were always among those most suspicious of Syria's intentions (rivaled only by the Christians). But Iran's regional domination of the Shi'ites by default provided Syria and Iran with the opportunity to fasten their grip over the Shi'ite communities in the south and in the Bekaa Valley—and to transform Lebanon into one of the most dangerous centers of international terror.

The grip on the Shi'ites of the south, known as the Jabal Amil Shi'ites, is politically important for Syria, both internally and externally. The hot conflict in southern Lebanon, waged by Syria through the pro-Iranian Hizballah movement, serves both to place pressure on the Israelis and to demonstrate to the Syrians domestically that the Syrian-Israeli conflict is still very much alive. As a Ba'thist, secular, Arab nationalist movement, the Syrian regime, just like the PLO before it, needs to mask its invasion of Lebanon and its repression there and at home. Hence the Syrian regime ostentatiously professes its commitment to a lofty external purpose—lest it be exposed as the 'Alawite tyranny it really is. Were the Shi'ites to withdraw from the conflict or to ally with the Israelis, then Syria would no longer have any rationale to continue its struggle against Zionism other than to regain the Golan Heights—which lie too close to Syria's capital for Assad's comfort. Ba'thism in Syria would be boxed in, eventually to crumble, much as Soviet communism did when it confronted insurmountable obstacles.

The other Shi'ite area, the Bekaa Valley, is also vitally important for both Syria and Iran. It has been transformed into the headquarters for counterfeiting, training, illegal drug-trafficking, indoctrination, and operations of all fundamentalist-based and pro-Syrian, secular Arab nationalist terror groups operating throughout the Middle East. It is from the Bekaa Valley that the bomb came that killed nineteen American servicemen in Dhahran. Lebanon-based terror is a major tool used by Iran and Syria to erode American prestige and regional presence. For the United States, any strategy that would compromise the eclipsing influence of Iran's revolutionary clerics over the Lebanese Shi'ites would usefully promote Western interests. Such a strategy would also begin to erode Syria's solid, Stalinistic occupation of Lebanon and would facilitate the restoration of Lebanon's sovereignty. Nominally, at least, such is the continuing policy goal of the United States.

Liberating the centers of learning in Najaf and Karbala in the wake of Saddam's demise would offer the region and the West a chance to recover the Shi'ite political structure from the *diktat* of Khomeini's narrow Shi'ite revolution—and to reinstate the traditional dynamic among Lebanon's Shi'ites. Prying the Lebanese Shi'ites away from a defunct Iranian Revolution and reacquainting them with the Iraqi Shi'ite community could significantly help to shift the region's balance and to whittle away at Syria's power. Without Iran's ideological domination of the Lebanese Shi'ites, Syria would loosen its grip on them. Syria's continued military presence would be exposed as a wrapping for the very same secular Arab nationalism so despised by these Shi'ites. A collapse of Iraq's Ba'thism could be the catalyst for the implosion of Assad's regime in Syria and, through the Shi'ite community, of the Islamic revolution in Iran as well.

Jordan understands the importance of this battleground in the general conflict. When Israel launched its Grapes of Wrath operation in Lebanon in April 1996, King Hussein hoped that Israel could undermine Syria's position in Lebanon by striking at Hizballah and Syrian targets, but not at the populations. The king had strongly criticized Syria for failing to prevent Lebanese bloodshed.[43] Israeli strategy was the opposite—that is, to push the Lebanese further into Syrian control, in the hope that Syria would shoulder the responsibility of bringing stability to the border area. When this strategy was later revealed, King Hussein began to criticize Israel.

Egypt

Egypt, the country that initiated the pan-Arabic nationalist wave in the post–World War II era with the rise of Nasser, not surprisingly came to

Syria's aid; it recognized that a triumph in Iraq for Jordan's King Hussein would spell defeat for pan-Arabic nationalism. Along with Syria, Egypt moved to sabotage Jordan's objective. Their strategy was simultaneously to prop up Saddam and to persuade the United States to pursue a narrow, Ba'thist coup rather than the broad-based insurrection favored by Jordan. Walid Qudayhah, an Egyptian intellectual closely affiliated with Mubarak's government, patriotically observed,

> Major countries are not inclined toward a Hashemite solution in Baghdad. A Hashemite presence will upturn the balances of power in favor of Iraq and Jordan against Syria. Egypt will view such a solution as a strong threat to its leadership role. . . . Qudhayhah considered another scenario to be likely—a scenario in which a coup is staged from within the regime. . . . Such a coup has to be staged by Tikriti Ba'thists from within the regime. They are the only force by virtue of their absolute control of the army. . . . Syria will be their ally.[44]

On September 3, 1995, President Hafez Assad flew to Egypt to meet with President Hosni Mubarak. The two reaffirmed that efforts to remove Saddam must remain pan-Arabic, and they accused Jordan of undermining inter-Arabic cooperation. Assad's next focus was on Iran. On September 10, Syrian foreign minister Farouq ash-Shar'a traveled to Iran to report to Ayatollah Rafsanjani that Syria had secured Egypt's complete support for the Syrian-Iranian policy on Iraq.[45] Parroting the views of Egypt's leaders, Cairo's government-run newspapers began harshly criticizing, even ridiculing, King Hussein and his Iraq policy. First came an article by Samir Ragab in Egypt's *al-Gomhuriya,* deriding Hussein as an American stooge.[46] Within days, almost all of Egypt's press echoed the same theme, as this editorial in *al-Akbar* exemplifies:

> The king is trying to exploit Iraq's predicament because it might prove opportune for reviving the dormant dream of the Hashemites to regain the throne of Baghdad and establish a united kingdom that links Jordan and Iraq, recover for the Hashemites some of that which they lost, complement the gulf states without considering their views and objectives and safeguard Israel and the West.[47]

Egypt and Syria were obviously worried about relations with the gulf states, especially Saudi Arabia, and about the damage that Jordan's initiative could inflict on their counter-bloc efforts if Jordan secured gulf support. As early as September 1995, *al-Wasat's* Damascus correspondent Ibrahim Hamidi reported, "[Syria's] main concern at present is the prospect of Jordan adopting a major role in bringing about a change in Iraq, which would reduce the oil-rich Gulf states' need for Syria."[48] This negative campaign continued well into 1996 and focused increasingly on the fear that Jordan would ally itself with the gulf state monarchies against Egypt and Syria. Jordan's anti-Saddam stance began to cause a rift between Riyadh and Damascus on regional policy.

Jordanian-Egyptian tensions intensified over the issue of Saudi-Jordanian ties, severely hindering Jordan's efforts in early 1996. Rapprochement with Saudi Arabia was strategically important for King Hussein for several reasons: Saudi Arabia was not a pan-Arabic nationalist nation, it had itself been the victim of Saddam Hussein, and it could be depended on to oppose reconciliation with Saddam Hussein's Iraq. In fact, Saudi Arabia could probably be depended on to support any serious effort to oust Saddam—which the Hashemites believed they offered.

Still, Hashemite-Saudi rivalries are old and cut deep. The Hashemites were historically the rulers of the Hejaz, which included Mecca, but they were driven from their ancestral domain by the armies of the advancing Saudi empire in the late 1920s. For the Hashemites, the Saudis were usurpers of the realm; for the Saudis, the Hashemites were irredentist claimants to the holiest part of the Saudi kingdom. Considering this history, it was extraordinarily momentous that Jordan and Saudi Arabia should have embarked on a path to reconciliation in late 1995 and early 1996.

In August 1995 Saudi Arabia welcomed Hussein Kamal's defection and King Hussein's new initiative. The editor of the pan-Arabic, Saudi-run weekly *al-Majalla* enthused in another Saudi daily, *Asharq al-Awsat*, on the positive role that Kamal could play in toppling Saddam, warning "opposition groups that if they try to discredit him they will only be assisting Saddam."[49] Indeed, the editor of a major Saudi newspaper wrote an editorial that blasted Syria, declaring that "the sudden emergence of Syrian-led opposition to the Jordanian project has unsettled many, and could end up rescuing the Iraqi regime from its grave predicament."[50] Saudi Arabia sent its intelligence director, Prince Turki al-Faisal, to Amman to debrief Kamal. The Saudis also invited Jordan's foreign minister, al-Kabariti, to come to Riyadh to meet with King Fahd. Saudi newspapers predicted "imminent, positive developments in the Saudi-Jordanian relationship," which had been severed since 1991.[51] While both the Saudis and the Jordanians quickly soured on Hussein Kamal himself, Jordanian-Saudi relations improved throughout the autumn of 1995. Diplomatic relations were reestablished in late 1995, with the appointment of Abdallah as-Sudairi as the new Saudi ambassador to Amman. Appointing an as-Sudairi established a sturdy link between Jordan and the as-Saud ruling family's Sudairi branch, which includes King Fahd and Princes Sultan, Naif, Turki, and Salman.

Matters went from bad to worse for Syria in early 1996. Assad must have been particularly disturbed when the Saudi ambassador to Jordan "declared that there are no differences between his country and Jordan over Iraq . . . and that the two countries were working together."[52] Assad's problem was compounded by the Jordanian "white revolution" in the first week of February 1996, installing al-Kabariti as prime minister—a man known for his antipathy toward Syria and his determination to depose Saddam Hussein.[53] Syria was in danger of losing Saudi support to Jordan on the Iraq issue.

Egypt, in concert with Syria, sought to undermine King Hussein.[54] Cairo moved quickly to help Assad not only in his campaign to discredit Hussein Kamal—which was irrelevant, since Kamal had already lost nearly all credibility as a positive catalyst for change in Baghdad—but to isolate and undermine Jordan as well. Egypt worked diligently to keep Saudi Arabia and Jordan apart. In early February, with much fanfare and two months of advance publicity, King Hussein was to travel to Saudi Arabia to meet with King Fahd and "seal the reconciliation between Jordan and Saudi Arabia."[55] In advance of this visit, Egypt worked behind the scenes with Crown Prince Abdallah of Saudi Arabia and Assad of Syria to persuade them to "clear the air with Iraq."[56] Only a few hours before King Hussein's trip, Mubarak flew to Riyadh and met with Abdallah. The two conspired to cancel the Fahd-Hussein summit and "to abort a full Jordanian-Saudi reconciliation at the last minute."[57] A number of Arab newspapers observed the next day that Jordan's Iraq policy was a central focus of the Mubarak-Abdallah meeting. The journalists noted that Mubarak met with Abdallah to "abort the Jordanian monarch's visit to the Kingdom by stressing that the call for a federation in Iraq [the Hashemite plan] was dangerous and could have an adverse impact on the stability of the region."[58] It worked: there was no Hussein-Fahd summit in early February 1996.

Nevertheless, Syria and Egypt could not completely derail the reconciliation between Saudi Arabia and Jordan. The summit occurred a few weeks later, and Jordanian-Saudi ties have continued to improve.

The Syrian Rapprochement with Iraq

Despite all of Syria's efforts and the assistance it received from Egypt and even from factions in Saudi Arabia, and despite the U.S. and Israeli strategic blunders of resurrecting the PLO and attempting to appease Syria, Jordanian efforts in support of an Iraqi insurrection continued to gain momentum until the spring of 1996. After a series of meetings between King Hussein and Iraqi National Congress leaders in London, the king called for a late-January conference in Amman that would encompass a broad array of opposition figures, including some that had previously been considered aligned with Syria and Iran.

Lacking the power to impede Jordan's efforts directly, Assad signaled that he and Iran would prefer a weak but still surviving Saddam to a Jordanian victory. Assad cautiously moved to bring Iraq into a coherent Iraqi-Syrian-Iranian-PLO axis—to prop up Saddam sufficiently to sabotage King Hussein's efforts. By early September 1995, Saudi newspapers were reporting:

> A new regional alliance is taking shape to counter U.S. plans for [Iraq]. . . . It is widely believed that Syria is . . . determined to wrench the "Iraqi card" from Jordan's hands and that Assad has even established contact with Saddam himself, his arch rival for two decades.[59]

In October, major Western newspapers began to report the rapprochement, saying that "the bitter foes of Baghdad suddenly decided that Saddam and the status quo were preferable to a potentially dangerous disintegration of Iraq," which is how King Hussein's objectives are generally described.[60] By mid-December, Arab newspapers commented on the improving Iraqi-Syrian ties. One Bahrain daily reported that "Syria is hinting that it might restore ties with Iraq in order to strengthen its hand."[61] Egypt played a major role in this effort as well.[62]

In early spring 1996, Syria began using Algerian mediation to effect a Syrian-Iraqi thaw.[63] By late spring, Assad reportedly began meeting with Saddam Hussein along the Syrian-Iraqi border, to forge

a common strategy against what Assad called "the return to the policy of alliances"—that is, the Jordanian efforts to overthrow Saddam
and create an Israeli-Jordanian-Turkish-American bloc.[64]

From August 1995 until early 1996, just when King Hussein
needed to muster all his assets as Saddam's regime floundered, Egypt
and Syria succeeded in diverting the king's attention. They obstructed
King Hussein's plans for insurrection in Iraq, and they supported Saddam Hussein diplomatically, and perhaps even financially, by facilitating his evasion of the sanctions against him. Egypt and Syria's vigorous efforts, in concert with American indulgence of these efforts,
have tremendously eroded American and Jordanian interests in Iraq.

7

The Strategic Centrality of Iraq

Defeating Saddam's regime in Iraq is critical for the United States. Our success affects both our international prestige and our strategic power in the Middle East. In part, Iraq demands American attention because of the aggressive and irresponsible nature of its regime. The nation threatens its adjacent neighbors and the entire region with its ambitions and with its brutal use and determined development of unconventional capabilities and long-range delivery systems. Moreover, Iraq's current government has inveterately used terrorism, making Saddam an international menace. Saddam Hussein sends agents to murder opposition figures throughout the world, detonates car bombs that kill scores of people, and attempts to provoke Arab-Israeli wars. He has tried to assassinate an American president (George Bush)—an outrage to which we decorously responded by lobbing several missiles at empty facilities.

Brutal and aggressive as Saddam's behavior is toward the outside world, though, the repression he inflicts on his own people is even more egregious. They are his first victims and his ultimate shield. Using them as hostages, Saddam exploits the humanity of the United States to paralyze our efforts to punish him. He is a calamity, and his removal has itself become a significant American interest.

Iraq's strategic importance to the United States, however, derives from a source beyond the pernicious, extortionist character of Saddam's regime. Because of Iraq's location, resources, population, and

connections with its neighbors, its eventual disposition merits our focused attention.

Geographically Propitious

A nation of 22 million, Iraq occupies some of the most strategically
blessed and resource-laden territory of the Middle East. It is a key
transportation route, and it is rich in both geographic endowments and
human talent. Its location on pathways between Asia and Europe, Africa and Asia, and Europe and Africa makes it an ideal route for armies, pipelines, and trade from both the eastern Mediterranean and
Asia Minor to the Persian Gulf. Iraq also has large, proven oil re-
serves, water, and other important resources. Its geographic centrality
and abundance of natural advantages alone make the country a regionally important center. On the basis of resources, power, and
wealth, Saddam's drive for regional hegemony before 1991 was ominous; with access to all his potential assets, he would be a hazard of
global dimension.

Beyond the vital consideration of the direct threat posed by Iraqi
weapons, the United States and its allies have been slow to acknowledge the strategic ramifications of Iraq's eventual political alignment.
Those who wish to damage U.S. interests, such as Russia, Iran, Syria,
and the Palestine Liberation Organization, have been far more adept
than we at crafting their policies toward Iraq in a strategic context. In
the months immediately following Desert Storm, only Syria and Iran
moved resolutely, albeit unsuccessfully, to undermine Saddam by trying to forge an Iraqi opposition under their tutelage. These efforts
failed because Syria lacked the assets to manipulate Iraqi politics as
easily as it manipulates those of the Lebanese. Eventually, Syria pursued a more limited goal: from 1995 onward, Syria and its ally Iran
have tried to dominate northern Iraq as a land bridge and as a springboard for their common efforts, with respect not only to Iraq but to Turkey and Jordan as well.

Perhaps more ominous is the recent formation of a new regional
strategic grouping that challenges the United States and its allies Jordan, Israel, and Turkey. A broad, quadrilateral rapprochement is
under way among Syria, Iran, the PLO, and Iraq. The PLO stands most
visibly, or at least candidly, in the vanguard of this diplomatic effort.
In late 1997, Yassir Arafat called for the formation of a new "eastern
front" that would include the four. Its purpose, he stated, was to chal-

lenge not only Israel but Turkey as well.[1] More worrisome, since it illustrates a regional trend, is the harsh, cold war, anti-American rhetoric espoused by the Palestinian Authority as it moves to parrot Saddam's oratory. For example, Arafat evoked some of the most provocative cold war imagery by praising the long-dead Sandinista revolution of Nicaragua as the model for the Palestinian revolution.[2]

In fact, some of the most vitriolic anti-American public incitement in the region comes from the PLO-appointed and -funded mufti of Jerusalem, Ikrim as-Sabri, and it is broadcast over Palestinian Authority television.[3] Much of his demogoguery is delivered in the context of support for Saddam's regime in its confrontation with the United States. The PLO also provides material support to Saddam by hunting down Iraqi opposition figures and by volunteering its facilities—including its embassy—in Iraq to hide plans and materials for Iraqi weapons of mass destruction safely out of the reach of UNSCOM inspectors.[4] In turn, Saddam tried to send Arafat $100 million in October 1997.[5] In July 1997 Saddam candidly described the Palestinian Authority as a strategic asset in his conflict with Israel.[6]

As the PLO—which has never severed its close ties with Iraq—labors to cobble together a new, anti-American regional bloc, Syria and Iraq are drawing closer together as well, much to the strategic detriment of Turkey and our other regional allies. In the summer of 1997, high-ranking Iraqi officials visited Damascus, the first such visit in decades. Egypt has also joined in this anti-Turkish crusade. In response, Jordan and Turkey have demonstrated some recognition (Jordan in late 1995, Turkey in 1996) of the necessity to influence Iraq's eventual disposition and form a counter-bloc, to avoid isolation and to pursue their strategic interests. Neither Israel nor the United States, however, seems to have acknowledged the region's strategic shift.

Iraq is the geopolitical pivot of these two regional blocs, and its destiny will determine which bloc will dominate the region. The emerging trend in this contest will sway fence-sitters such as Saudi Arabia and Egypt, eager to divine and align with the winners. The longer Iraq remains under Saddam's control and the more his power revives, the brighter the prospects and stronger the resilience and appeal of the anti-Western axis.

The fragility of the Middle Eastern nations, with their unrepresentative, undemocratic governance, is the key to the competitive struggle. Considering also the cross-border alliances of tribes, sects, and clans that still define Levantine politics, the strategic contest over

Iraq affects the course of internal politics among all of Iraq's neighbors. Thus, internal political developments in Iraq can lead to a dramatic shift in the Middle East's strategic balance. Defeat in this competition can bring down some of the regimes engaged, including Syria's Ba'thist, Iran's Islamic, or Jordan's Hashemite government.

Such dramatic shifts in the local balance of power eventually affect Russian plans as well. In fact, the strategic vacuum that the United States is leaving in the Levant has already begun to attract Russia's interest and intervention. Russia's prime minister, Yevgeny Primakov, launched a rather effective effort when he was foreign minister to assist Saddam's obstruction of the inspections program in the 1997 and 1998 crises. This effort was part of a larger Russian initiative to challenge the U.S. position in the region. Since early 1997, Russia has been actively trying not only to arm but also to forge a strategic bloc among nations located along a thousand-mile strategic arc—including Serbia, Cyprus, Syria, Iraq, and Iran—in large part to isolate Turkey. These Russo-Arab efforts were accelerated in 1998, and they have been assisted by the European Union's antagonistic policies toward Turkey, which weaken and complicate Turkey's ties to the West and to NATO.

Iraq lies at the center of this "bloc competition" between Russia and an oblivious United States. When we welcomed Russian mediation in our disputes with Iraq, in effect we became an accomplice in the effort to disassemble our own strategic scaffolding in the region. Russia intervened not as a neutral enforcer of UN resolutions but rather as Iraq's mentor and protector. Iraq's disposition, about which Russia has now as much to say as has the United States, will determine whether it will be Turkey and Jordan or Iran and Syria that become marginalized and assailed. The battle to define and dominate Iraq is the battle to prevail as the leading power in the Levant. It is within the framework of this larger initiative that we should heed Yassir Arafat's 1997 boasts about forming a bloc to counter Turkey and Israel, and his tribute to the Sandinista revolution. Ultimately this is the struggle to determine whether America will remain the predominant external power in the region or will sadly go the way of Britain in the 1940s and 1950s—home.

The Significance of Northern Iraq

Every conflict contains a battle over a key territory endowed with strategic significance. The great early nineteenth-century military strategist Carl von Clausewitz called this territory the "center of gravity." Its loss, he observed, first exposes one of the adversaries and then breaks that party's political will to sustain the struggle. The battle over this special territory becomes the proving ground of the combatants' respective wills to win, and its resolution the watershed for the entire conflict. In the fall of 1995, the safe haven in northern Iraq became that center of gravity for the multiple expressions of the Iraq conflict: the Hashemites versus the pan-Arabic nationalists; the Iraqi National Congress versus Saddam Hussein; the United States versus Saddam Hussein; the Jordanians versus the Syrians; King Hussein versus Iraqi Ba'thism; and even the United States versus itself, our clarity of purpose contraposing against our irresoluteness. Pointlessly, the United States did what none of our opponents could have done: we abandoned the north, so as to pursue an illusory coup.

Northern Iraq was crucial for the success of the INC's insurgency strategy. The territory was not merely a geographical springboard for attack; after all, the insurgency could have been launched from land situated in any of Iraq's neighbors. Far more important, the INC's presence in northern Iraq was essential for the idea it represented: a liberated slice of Iraq under the leadership of a properly functioning, coherent, and indigenous government.

The United States needs to build some form of provisional Iraqi government as a base of support on the ground and to establish it in a territorial entity from which it can incrementally extend its control— reassembling the fragments of the collapsed tyrannical state along the way. Otherwise, a Somalia- or Yugoslavia-like, warlord-ridden anarchy will ensue in the aftermath of a coup—much to the detriment of such regional allies as Turkey, Jordan, and Israel, much to the benefit of such regional foes as Iran and Syria.

This is the concept behind the formation of the Iraqi National Congress—a provisional government ensconced in northern Iraq that serves as a unified umbrella for all opposition factions and steadily whittles away at Saddam's regime territorially while simultaneously, relentlessly undermining it ideologically. It is imperative that we support the INC's pursuit of a fundamental change in Iraq—for its own merit, and to avoid the prospect of northern Iraq, and eventually all of Iraq, becoming a power vacuum like Lebanon.

Maintaining the status quo—or transferring power to another Ba'thist regime—will inexorably result in the disintegration of Iraq. Failure to establish a coherent provisional government in northern

Iraq leaves the entire nation vulnerable to the designs of Syria and Iran, which opportunistically seek to extend their influence into the growing chaos. That is what happened in 1995, when the safe haven collapsed as a result of the American betrayal of the INC. Both Syria and Iran intervened and became the dominant forces there, transforming the zone into a Lebanese-style dominion and distending their power to menace the entire region.[7]

To prevail over Syrian and Iranian power and to sabotage their schemes in northern Iraq, the United States must reengage the INC. Syrian and Iranian influence can best be limited by establishing an alternative provisional government that opposes Saddam and is sympathetic to the West—much like the Polish government-in-exile that operated out of London during World War II. Such a government could preempt Syria and Iran by collecting the pieces of Iraq as they splinter. It would suffuse the vacuum that Syria and Iran eagerly seek to exploit.

Because of the INC's importance to King Hussein's opposition to Saddam and because of its geographic base of power, northern Iraq became the key battleground between the two emerging regional blocs: the revolutionary challengers to the traditional Arab and Muslim elite, centered on Iraq, the PLO, Syria, and Iran, all hostile to the West; and the alternative bloc, centered on Jordan, Turkey, and Israel, all aligned with the West. Syria and Iran have been trying to sabotage King Hussein and to complicate his attempts to work with the INC by establishing their hegemony over northern Iraq, and their efforts have been abetted by the collapse of America's role in the safe haven area.

In the summer of 1995, at about the same time as Jordan began to challenge Iraq, the United States mediated a cease-fire among Kurdish factions in northern Iraq, known as the Dublin agreement. This was a blow to Syria and Iran, not only because the previous combat had offered those nations an opportunity to choose sides and acquire allies among the Kurds, but also because the agreement designated the INC as the protector of peace in northern Iraq. The agreement thus restored the organization's credibility and potency, redeeming it as an effective force after its period of disarray in the aftermath of Kurdish infighting in spring 1995.

The Dublin agreement cast the INC as the focal point of all policy in northern Iraq and laid a solid geographic foundation for Jordan to pursue its Hashemite initiative. Once the agreement was signed, however, the United States simply walked away from the opportunity we had created. We did not use the Dublin agreement to strengthen and promote the INC as a solution to the Iraq problem or to solidify our position in northern Iraq. While U.S. envoys promised economic, financial, and security assistance to the INC, little in fact materialized. Without U.S. involvement, the working relations between the two main Kurdish factions deteriorated, as the INC lost its mediating effectiveness.

Three developments ensued after the summer of 1995: the United States neglected northern Iraq; Iran and Syria took advantage of U.S. inattentiveness and their own proximity to assert their influence; and Iran moved (in mid-October) to supplant the INC as the chief mediator among the various Kurdish factions. In response to these developments, Assistant Secretary of State Robert Pelletreau was blasé. He opined that these developments lacked strategic significance—and that any attempt to bring stability to Iraq's northern zone should be appreciated.[8]

The Kurdish factions diverged in three directions. The PUK fell under Iranian influence and the KDP under Turkish—a reliable recipe for competition. The PKK remained an Iranian- and Syrian-run organization, with little indigenous following.

Two weeks after the U.S.-brokered Dublin agreement, the PKK attacked its pro-INC Kurdish rivals in an effort to reignite inter-Kurdish conflict among the two main indigenous Kurdish factions, the PUK and the KDP. Since the United States had already decided that northern Iraq was a sideshow, if not a burden, to our main efforts to foment a coup in Baghdad, we failed to grasp the significance and strategy behind the attack. The region's inhabitants, however, were quick to discern that Syria was steering events in a particular direction. Arab newspapers broadly understood the PKK's attack as part of the effort to derail the INC and the American plans for Iraq. For example, Kamran Karadaghi, *al-Hayat's* commentator on Iraqi issues, noted that the attack was

> part of efforts to undermine U.S. influence in the enclave . . . which could be part of the broader rivalry between Washington and Damascus over the Iraqi opposition and post-Saddam Iraq. The PUK-KDP agreement [the August 1995 U.S.-brokered Dublin agreement] provides for the INC to play a major role in policing the truce between them, and this runs counter to Syria's attempts to supplant the INC with an Iraqi opposition coalition under its auspices aimed at thwarting what it sees as the "American project" for Iraq's future.[9]

What many observers failed to see, however, was that the United States did not care; we had already abandoned northern Iraq and the INC.

Throughout the fall of 1995, Iran and Syria pressed both the KDP and the PUK to acknowledge them as the main power brokers. Iran moved the Supreme Assembly of the Islamic Republic of Iraq's military wing, the Badr forces, into northern Iraq by December—an act that prompted concern from Turkey, but not from the United States.[10]

The PUK, located in the eastern part of the enclave, buckled first and came to terms with Iran. The KDP, located in the western part, remained aloof and refused to disband its anti-Iranian wing, the KDP-Iran. By the spring of 1996, Iran's Revolutionary Guards were intervening directly and freely in northern Iraq—an aggression that still drew no American response. The KDP was overwhelmed by Iran's pressure.[11] In June 1996 Iran invaded northern Iraq, and it pressed the PUK into active hostility against the KDP. The United States offered no response to these developments, further demonstrating our political disengagement from northern Iraq.

Iran and Syria succeeded by the summer of 1996 in forcing Kurdish factions in the north to submit to Iran and Syria's domination, on pain of annihilation. This outcome was a direct result of the U.S. abandonment of the Iraqi National Congress and the northern Iraqi safe haven. It represented not merely a policy lapse, but rather a policy reversal. The United States had jettisoned the goal of eroding Saddam's power incrementally through a resistance army.[12] Instead, through the CIA we shifted our support to the *Wifaq*, in the hope that it could find a general or a colonel close to Saddam who would launch a coup. The dangerous strategic vacuum in the north that we expected to leave could safely be filled, we assumed, by a new Ba'thist regime in Baghdad with the arrival of the fabled coup. Of course, this coup never materialized; the United States had set itself up for defeat.

Picking Up the Pieces in Turkey, Jordan, and Iraq

The abandonment of the northern safe haven profoundly affected the competition among blocs, not only because it undermined the INC-Jordanian cooperation but also because it threatened Turkey. Yassir Arafat was revelatory in describing the purpose of his 1997 strategic initiative to form a PLO-Syria-Iraq-Iran axis: primarily to challenge Turkey and Jordan, only secondarily to challenge Israel.[13] Syria, the

PLO, and Egypt have devoted much of their energies since 1996 to trying to derail the thriving military alliances between Jordan and Turkey and between Israel and Turkey.

The U.S. retreat, leaving Syria and Iran to assume a dominant role in northern Iraq, undermines the strategic interests of Turkey, Jordan, and Israel. We have allowed Syria and Iran to exploit the resulting chaos and to establish a more potent base from which the PKK could strike Turkey, whose strategic place is defined by the Kurdish conflicts and by the Syrian-Iranian exploitation of these conflicts to destabilize it.

In early 1997 Turkey invaded the northern Iraq zone, both to combat terrorism and to stem the unchecked surge of Iran, Syria, and Iraq into that power vacuum. But over the long run, Turkey will find it impossible to cope with PKK terror unless it strikes and sustains an effort against the sources of that terror in Syria, Syrian-controlled Lebanon, and Iran. Unable or unwilling to do so as this book goes to press in autumn 1998, Turkey has chosen to work with the KDP against the other Kurdish factions. Turkey believes that the PUK is unwilling to rein in the PKK because of the PUK's dependency on Iran. This belief is unhappily true, but not because the PUK is inherently pro-PKK; rather, the opportunity created by the weakening of the INC in northern Iraq has driven the PUK into Iran's hands. As long as the Kurdish areas are under the protective umbrella of either Syria or Iran, the Kurds will be in no position to assert an independent policy that accords with Turkey's national interests. While the PUK is isolated and forced to accept Iran as its lifeline, it will be unable to defy its benefactor and root out the well-endowed PKK infrastructure residing in its territory.

Working with any one of the Kurdish factions in isolation embroils Turkey in internal Kurdish rivalries. Ultimately, Turkey may find itself with only one option: to establish a coherent, indigenous authority in northern Iraq that will help secure the Turkish-Iraqi border. From the standpoint of terror, any of Turkey's neighbors—Syria, Iran, or Saddam's Iraq—could establish control over the border, and it is likely that all these actors will offer Turkey such an option. But while acceptance of such an offer might ameliorate the terror problem, it would also constitute strategic defeat for both Turkey and the West. In fact, it was precisely to create such a trade-off—restraining terrorists in exchange for strategic surrender—that Syria and Iran employed terror against Turkey in the first place.

Rewarding terrorism—obviously a strategic mistake in any case —in this way would promote the success of anti-Western forces in filling the power vacuum. Such forces, by extension, seek relentlessly to weaken the West's regional allies. Turkey could secure some calm in the short term by acceding to Syrian, Iranian, or Iraqi blackmail, but doing so would ensure a much graver danger in the long term.[14] That is why Iran and Syria have for years focused on consolidating their power in northern Iraq by whittling away at Turkey's regional stature, as well as at the stature of Jordan and the United States.[15]

The only way for Turkey to establish a coherent, indigenous authority in northern Iraq would be to encourage and shield the INC. Turkish assistance could resurrect the INC as the chief power broker in northern Iraq. In turn, the INC would undertake to coordinate a pan-Kurdish effort to control the Turkish-Iraqi border, as it did under the Dublin agreement; to expel Iran and Syria from the north; and to bring an end to the PKK's war on Turkey. The benefits would be mutual. While Turkey could use its ties to the INC to quell its inter-Kurdish rivalries, the INC could use Turkey for its linkage with the West, as well as to counterbalance Syrian, Iranian, and Ba'thist Iraqi power. Turkey is thus a key ally in the joint Jordanian-INC effort to defeat Saddam and the Syrian-Iranian-PLO bloc.

In the context of coinciding Jordanian and Turkish interests and activities in Iraq, it is worth noting that Ankara and Amman are cooperating openly, with strategic agreements and joint military exercises. Moreover, Jordan was careful not to criticize Turkey when Turkey invaded northern Iraq in early 1997. In fact, Jordan's Crown Prince Hassan traveled to Ankara only days after the invasion, and he spoke warmly of deepening Turkish-Jordanian strategic ties. Such ties are especially important in the framework of rapidly developing Turkish-Israeli strategic cooperation. Considering all these initiatives, the West is encouragingly close to enjoying the emergence of a tightly bonded Turkish-INC-Jordanian-Israeli bloc that could eclipse other blocs and stabilize the entire Levant.

Toward Defeat

The absence of a visible U.S. strategy on Iraq and the retreat from northern Iraq was read by all observers, both in the Middle East and here at home, as signaling U.S. political disengagement from that country. Sanctions on Iraq began effectively to ease, as the international coalition necessary to maintain them disintegrated. In late 1996 Syria initiated contact with Iraq, and by 1998 it was allowing Iraq's contraband oil to pass through the Syrian border. Between 1996 and 1998 many members of the coalition that had sacrificed their economic interests in Iraq in deference to American leadership—under the assumption that America was committed to removing Saddam— lost their patience. Confidence in American leadership waned as we surrendered the policy-setting initiative to an amorphous, rudderless international community. As economic pressures to abandon sanctions mounted and as America's efforts grew more sporadic and lackadaisical and our determination to remove Saddam questionable, Iraq's neighbors, some of our European allies, and even the Arab states most threatened by Saddam began to seek their peace with Baghdad. Saddam Hussein perceptively sensed the diminution of America's regional stature. He challenged the UN and the United States directly in late 1997, and he exposed the truth—that the United States no longer commanded an international following, and that we lacked the determination to use military force unilaterally.

8

Defeating Despotism

For most of this century, Arab politics has been tumultuous because of the conflict between the traditional establishment and revolutionary upheaval. This tension first surfaced during the Great Arab Revolt against the Ottomans in World War I, led by the Hashemite Sherif Hussein of Mecca. Sharif Hussein stood for the old Arabic landed, feudal aristocracy, but the rank and file of his followers included a new revolutionary group of Arab officers, many of whom were educated in the West or in Western schools. After the war and the capitulation of Turkey, their common enemy, these diametrically opposed factions of Arab society commenced a conflict that continues to the present day. It is a conflict that resembles, and was in fact informed by, the upheaval that gripped European politics in the age of modernity, and the French rather than the American revolution is its model. In both Europe and the Middle East since the end of the nineteenth century, radical efforts have continuously challenged traditional society; utopian, statist, and arrogant political movements have replaced burgeoning ones that were more liberal, decentralized, and humble. Thus the politics of the Arab world and the anti-American sentiment so prevalent there can insightfully be viewed as an emulation of the revolutionary upheaval and spirit of totalitarianism that began in Europe two centuries ago.

The crisis in Iraq reflects the deeply troubled waters roiled by traditional Arab Islamic society's incompatibility with revolutionary movements, both secular and religious. The United States has haplessly drifted into these waters ill equipped. Our fear of the dissolution of Iraq and our hope for a smooth transfer of power from Saddam to a military dictatorship have generated a policy that embraces the wrong team in the contest. The great conflict of the Middle East is that between the bloc system sought by Arafat, Saddam, and Assad and the alternative configuration advocated by King Hussein and the Iraqi National Congress. It is the twilight struggle between the two mighty forces of the Great Arab Revolt that helped liberate the Arabs from the Ottomans.

At the center of the maelstrom is Ahmad Chalabi and the Iraqi National Congress. He, his family, and the organization he created represent an older Iraq and a traditional elite that have been battered, oppressed, and enslaved by pan-Arabic nationalist governments for forty years. Even in the last years of Iraqi Hashemite rule, that older aristocracy was besieged; in the futile hope of appeasing their adversaries' hostility, the Hashemites caved in too readily to pan-Arabic nationalist demands.

Tradition must be acknowledged as the reference point for change. Edmund Burke, a man of conservative core who was in fact an advocate of reform, observed the devastation wrought by the French Revolution. He wrote incisively on the interdependency between tradition and change in a healthy society:

> A state without the means of some change is without the means of conservation. . . . [When] nations had lost the bond of union in their ancient edifice, they did not, however, dissolve the whole fabric. On the contrary . . . they regenerated the deficient part of the old constitution through parts which were not impaired. . . . When the legislature altered the direction, but kept the principle, they showed that they held it inviolable.
>
> The gentlemen of the Society for Revolutions see nothing . . . but the deviation from the constitution; and they take deviation from the principle for the principle. They have little regard for the obvious consequences of their doctrine, though they must see that it leaves positive authority in very few of the positive institutions in this country.
>
> Ill would our ancestors . . . have deserved their fame for wisdom if they had found no security for their freedom but in rendering their government feeble in its operations

and precarious in its tenure; if they had been able to contrive no better remedy for arbitrary power than civil confusion.[1]

To return the country to its former stability, the remnants of that older Iraq must be restored to power. And the Hashemites still have a role to play in facilitating the reconstitution of Iraqi society.

Watershed Summer of 1995

The course that politics will take in Iraq is still undetermined. The summer of 1995 began an era that must be a watershed for Middle Eastern politics. The efforts of the INC in spring 1995 delivered a grave blow not only to the tyrant Saddam Hussein but also to Ba'thist tyranny. The INC had embarked on an initiative to restore Iraqi politics to an indigenous, traditional leadership that included the Shi'ites, to operate eventually under the Hashemite umbrella. King Hussein recognized that Saddam's precarious control and the INC's triumphs offered the Hashemites an opportunity to cripple the pan-Arabic nationalist orthodoxy dominating Arab politics since the 1950s. To redeem Ba'thism and stem the forces of restoration, Ba'thist Syria and Iraq would have to sabotage King Hussein and the INC. And so they did.

The contest operates on a number of levels: to oust Saddam Hussein; to tilt the region's balance of power between pan-Arabic nationalism and the Hashemites; to elect absolute or decentralized power; to persevere in the arrogant politics of modernity or to return to the tempered politics of tradition and evolutionary change. These struggles have hung in the balance since 1995. All roads have led to Iraq—and specifically, to northern and western Iraq. The battle over these regions' fate will prove either to be the Hashemites' Agincourt, a stunning underdog victory from which Saddam Hussein cannot recover, or the fields of the Horns of Hittim, the beginning of the end of Hashemite power in the Middle East.

Since early 1996 the tide of battle has been turning in Saddam's favor, largely as a result of the U.S. decision to change our policy in 1995. Neither Syria's intrigues nor Egypt's disruptions nor the PLO's subversion nor Saddam's wily brutality succeeded in sabotaging the joint Jordanian-INC effort. Even the reentry of Russia in the equation, with its pro-Saddam foreign minister (and now prime minister) Yevgeny Primakov, failed to tip the balance. The damage was done by U.S.

foreign policy. From 1992 to 1995 we supported the INC and maintained a robust safe haven in northern Iraq, providing hopeful opportunities for the INC, King Hussein, and ourselves. In mid-1995 the United States suddenly shifted policy and sided with the pan-Arabic nationalist bloc, accepting its propaganda regarding the Shi'ite menace, the breakup of Iraq, and the need to centralize tyranny. And so we turned to the *Wifaq*.

The nation of Jordan is now squeezed from three sides—by the PLO, Syria, and Iraq. The Iraqi National Congress, although not destroyed completely, was deeply harmed by Saddam's invasion of northern Iraq. The Hashemite monarchy of Jordan and the INC now face the battles of their lives—to be won or lost as much in Washington's corridors as in Baghdad's alleys.

Reversing U.S. Policy

The United States calibrated its policy to maintain the territorial cohesiveness of Iraq under a strong central government, even if such a government were significantly repressive. We believed that Saddam Hussein could best and most safely be deposed by our conspiring with the *Wifaq*, a collection of high-ranking Sunni, Ba'thist defectors led by Iyad 'Alawi and General Nuri. Because we focused so narrowly on maintaining the centralized unity of Iraq, we dreaded the long-term effects of successfully protecting a safe haven; the existence of such a zone encouraged centrifugal tendencies that could surpass our control in the wake of decentralization. We also feared that robust protection of the safe haven would contradict our efforts to encourage a coup because, according to the prevailing wisdom, such a haven discouraged military officers close to Saddam. In short, the United States assumed that the safe haven in northern Iraq and the INC's insurgency plan endangered our own supreme objective for the region: stability. As in 1991, we pursued an illusory military coup at the cost of an actual insurgency.

The successful efforts of the INC in 1995 had left Saddam precious little at that critical juncture; only the U.S. decision to abandon the safe haven saved him. The gulf war was thus being lost in late 1995 and early 1996, as on the eve of success we squandered a four-year effort to overthrow Saddam and install a new, decentralized, and more traditional regime in Baghdad.

The words of one U.S. ambassador who served in the Persian

Gulf from 1994 to 1997 best exemplify what has gone wrong in U.S. policy, and why the United States is losing the war against Saddam:

> [Saddam Hussein] can now pose credibly as the champion of a Sunni Iraq against a U.S. government that wants to use Kurdish and Shi'ite Arab separatism to weaken the regime in Baghdad. All the Arab states are Sunni. . . . Under these circumstances, the United States is fast on its way to losing Arab support. . . . There is a way to rebuild coalition support, both inside and outside the Arab world. . . . We must say clearly and forcefully that we will deal sympathetically with Iraq, immediately upon Saddam Hussein's departure. . . . If we must hold our noses while we do all this with a thuggish new regime in Iraq, so be it. . . . Threatening covert action and military attacks, as we are doing, traps the worried men around Saddam Hussein into supporting him more determinedly. Saddam Hussein can say to them, quite convincingly, that after he is gone, they are all lost. Iraq will divide . . . and the minority Sunnis will be hounded. A policy that calls for a new Iraqi government—implicitly, a Sunni one—and restores Iraq to strength has great potential for giving those around Saddam Hussein a way out.[2]

According to David Ransom, American interest is best served by seeking a Sunni-dominated, centralized military regime in Iraq to replace Saddam, even if such a regime is "thuggish." Sadly, this is the concept that underlay the grave miscalculation of Saddam that we made before 1990.

The Middle East Foreign Policy Community

What has happened in Iraq is not an isolated policy failure; it reflects the failure of the reigning assumptions in Western (first British, then U.S.) policy toward the region since the early 1920s. The policy is to pursue a coup rather than a broad-based insurgency and to prefer a diminished Ba'thist Iraq under Saddam over chaos, since such an entity would still serve as a bulwark against the Islamic Republic of Iran. But this plan and our earlier policy of supporting Saddam against Iran both derive from a fundamental flaw in the way U.S. policy makers view the Middle East: an inability to recognize evil and the inherent menace of totalitarian tyranny, whether cloaked in religious or in secular garb.

Much of American policy toward the Middle East has been guided by four assumptions. The first is that Middle Eastern politics is exotic and therefore exempt from the influences of Western thought, both in its deviant and in its enlightened forms. Second, this exotic aspect of Middle Eastern politics must be overcome, as the thinking goes, since the primitive influences of tribalism and local forms of identity—all forms of political decentralization—threaten to create instability and to break up states. Such breakups in the Arab world would signify disaster, according to the received wisdom. Third, the effort to forge stable nations from such numerous, "primitive" particles explains, if not necessitates, the excessive repression and aggression of radical despotism. Fourth, anti-Americanism and anti-Zionism are motivated by anticolonialism. All four of these assumptions are false.

While Arab society over the past millennium has certainly been plagued by incessant tribal, familial, and clan violence along with infamous corruption, the intensification of violence over the past seventy years represents a qualitative change. Much of the lethality comes not from the traditional aspects of Arab culture and its factionalized nature, but rather from the influence of radical European trends—totalitarianism striving to transform society. In the Middle East, the revolutionary impulse has dominated for seventy years, and the prevailing form of government has been republican tyranny.

Further, the vast majority of violence in the Middle East is internal to Arab nations; in other words, the real war is that waged by nations against their own citizens. It results from the rise within the Arab world of men whose politics focuses on the effort to wipe out all forms of traditional leadership and political decentralization. Such men have introduced Arab nations to the brutal ideologies that informed communism, fascism, and other totalitarian movements. Their politics has allowed the most ambitious to intensify age-old blood feuds and squabbles among families, factions, clans, and tribes—always present, but hitherto maintained at a low boil. Now the simmering hostilities have erupted in the use of poison gas and mass murder.

Ultimately, utopian attempts to alter society are destined to fail, leaving the region plagued by confused identities. Failed states that dabbled in totalitarian politics are inherently driven to lash out at symbols of freedom, and particularly at America. Arab politics can best be understood by returning to two bodies of Western political literature. The first deals with the despotism and tyranny that preceded the growth of liberalism in the eighteenth century and then returned, following the rise of totalitarian politics in the nineteenth and twentieth centuries. The second deals with the phenomenon of the angry revolutionary in Europe, and especially in Russia.

U.S. policy toward the Middle East, regrettably, is not informed by a recognition of the inherently destructive and anti-American nature of tyranny. Instead we have tended to dismiss the violence and instability of the region as unavoidably deriving from the backwardness of the Levant, and have looked to modernity, statism, and centralized power as a solution.

Western intellectuals and policy makers have accepted the propaganda of pan-Arabic nationalists, who claim that such radical statism is "progressive" and is necessary to modernize and homogenize the primordial loyalties of primitive, factionalized peoples. More important, we consider radical statism to be the only path to development that brings stability. Thus U.S. policy makers ignore the links between violence, instability, and external aggression on the one hand and tyrants' appeals to spuriously noble causes on the other. Their repression easily assumes sectarian or ethnic characteristics and tears asunder the tenuous cohesiveness of fragile nations. Moreover, U.S. policy makers fail to appreciate that totalitarianism does not lead ultimately to the formation of unified entities; rather, it implacably gives rise to the very chaos and national breakdowns we so wished to avert. It produces failed states. American policy counterproductively encourages the most dangerous trends in Arab politics. It also contradicts our policy initiatives in other parts of the world, which are based on advancing democracy, freedom, and the decentralization of all forms of power—all the elements of both classic liberalism and conservative change.

Neither a robust U.S. policy nor a continued presence is the cause of regional anti-American hostility; this animus emerges, rather, from the internal character of totalitarian regimes. The traditional leadership of the Middle East rebelled against the Ottoman empire but welcomed and cooperated with the British and even the Zionists, whom they viewed as a brotherly national movement. But radical, Western-educated members of the Arab community (many of whom lived in Paris, others of whom attended Western-run local schools) became hostile because of their exposure to the leftist political ideas surging through Europe at the turn of the century. Such revolutionaries were energized by their antipathy toward the region's traditional leadership. Encouraged by the radical foreign movements of nazism and then communism, these politicians seized power and exploited anti-Western demagoguery to justify their ambitious internal repression. They shrewdly appealed to the defense of a higher cause—the nation, the race, pan-Arabism, Communist revolution, and eventually pan-Islamism. Craven, fawning Western politicians—from Britain's Lord Alfred Milner to current U.S. policy makers—inadvertently lent credence to the demagoguery and paved the way for these revolutionaries' rise to power.

Once such men had secured power, excessive repression became a patriotic virtue in their societies—a noble resistance against the insidious threat of imperialism. The putative "anticolonialism" decried by pan-Arabic nationalist and pan-Islamic fundamentalist movements echoed the "anti-imperialism" call of Lenin. Citizenship became synonymous with mobilization for the higher cause; treason, with any call for the diminution of centralized power; and justice, with regime-employed terror. Anti-Americanism and anti-Zionism came to be the battle cry of tyrants at war with their own people.

Regrettably, U.S. policy on Iraq—like U.S. policies applied more broadly toward the Middle East—reflects the effectiveness with which local pan-Arabic nationalist politicians have sold their narrowly factional, radical agenda to our injudicious and gullible regional specialists. This unfortunate choice of the wrong side has characterized our policies toward Lebanon and the Palestinians as well. We are gulled by erroneous assertions about the evils of Arab Shi'ism and by the oft-chanted mantra of the "danger" of the breakup of Arab states that would follow the decentralization of power.

By accepting the despots' views of the region's problems, U.S. regional policy, like the British policy that preceded it, tolerates and even encourages the very radicalism that has led elsewhere in the world to the deadliest century in human history. Our policy reflects our self-deprecating attitude of embarrassment over Western ideas, culture, traditions, and power, along with a deferential effort to display our anticolonial credentials. We have been eager to support statist centralization of power and the seemingly "progressive," though in fact despotic, attempts to transform Arab society. The United States has consistently undermined our friends and betrayed our values in the Middle East. The fruits of our policy are a weakening of our influence over and respect from the region's inhabitants. Our continuing regional failure has served to vindicate rather than to discredit the politics of tyranny. And our regional position has eroded over the past decades, despite our cold war and Persian Gulf War victories.

To Decentralize Power

At the heart of totalitarianism is the centralization of power and the severing of the bands of civil society—those forms of authority that stand between the government and the individual. Values such as patriotism, honor, and virtue, which must come from the population itself in a healthy society, have been arrogated by the state and its tyrannical leaders to serve their narrow personal interests. The personal world of the individual has been confiscated by the public realm of the state; peoples are enslaved by their governments. All vestiges of tradition, power, religion, identity, and culture that obstruct the radical transformation are attacked. If possible, they are expropriated by the state as an extension of its power; if not, they are eliminated. Those who resist enslavement are declared "enemies of the people" and engulfed by a policy of terror. The Arab world has been devastated by utopian movements, leaving its nations in shards and anarchy.

The United States must dramatically break away from this destructive course and instead select allies from among those who seek to change the nature of Arab politics—not toward another radical utopian idea that aims at transforming human nature and loyalties,[3] but rather toward the traditional patterns of power and ancient loyalties, upon which more stable societies can be built. The Middle East needs a conservative restoration along the lines advocated by Edmund Burke. U.S. policy toward Iraq should establish a new regional emphasis on decentralization of power to replace the tyrannical, ideological politics of the twentieth century with community leaderships. And Iraqis need to determine which elements of their traditions can serve as the reference point for change in the future.

Such a policy can begin with the Iraqi National Congress. The INC is not a faction: it is the coalition of factional alliances who agreed to cooperate, to construct a common defense against the tyrannical Iraqi government. For the United States and other Western nations this notion should be familiar. It is the concept by which modern Western civilization came into being. Nations emerged from the prolonged alliance of factions under one protective but unintrusive umbrella leadership. Governments informed by this concept served, rather than subdued or erased, the common interests of factions—of feudal lords in medieval Europe, of tribes, sects, and clans in the Middle East today. Such governments over time forged a territorial concept of community and nation around limited government.

Perspectives

Discussion of the Iraq problem must necessarily involve a reexamination of the basic principles of U.S. foreign policy. Like our Middle East policy as a whole, our Iraq policy has been considered in isolation of the principles for which America stands—particularly, the principle of recognizing the damages of tyranny and the benefits of limited, decentralized government. Western nations should embrace the concept of forging states in harmony with, rather than in contradiction to, our own successful experience: the stable and free nations are all rooted in the commitment to limited government, diffused power, and politics shaped to suit men as they are, rather than how they might become, if their natures could be radically and violently altered.

Any effort to deal coherently with Iraq, with the strategic balance in the Levant, and with anti-Americanism in the region must begin with a determination to defeat the destructive politics of pan-Arabism in Iraq. An effective strategy must recognize this necessity, and it must reject all forms of pan-Arabic nationalism as legitimate or productive forces in Arab politics. Our failure to remove the pan-Arabic nationalist mantras from our policy making has consistently wrought our exaggerated concern for the preservation of a minority, Sunni-based regime that excludes and represses Kurds and Shi'ites—driving both into Iran's hands. Usefully, we should instead concern ourselves with the creation of a loosely unified Iraqi confederal government, shaped around strong sectarian and provincial entities.

No possible solution to the Iraq problem can be premised on the concept that the Sunni core of Iraq matters exclusively in defining that country. The Sunni residents and all of Iraq's citizens must be severed from the destructive regional agenda that ensures a fractionalized Iraq and fails to establish even the minimal sense of community from which a solid and eventually free, liberal nation could emerge.

For this reason, all schemes of palace coups, assassinations, and conspiracies to overthrow Saddam with a view toward achieving an alternative, pan-Arabic nationalist regime are futile and contrary to American interests. Even if such a conspiracy were to succeed in toppling Saddam, it would only return Iraq to the same misery it now suffers. It would also forfeit the opportunity to strike a mortal blow against the Iranian revolution and to undermine the other Ba'thist threat in the region, Syria.

The goal of ridding Iraq of Saddam by way of a coup and that policy's underlying assumptions should be reexamined. Saddam is nearly coup-proof; there is no silver-bullet, cost-free way to depose him. He is a far better conspirator than the CIA—more resolute, more wily, more brutal. Only an insurgency may be able to defeat Saddam, by exploiting the weakness and demoralized state of his conventional army.

Were the United States to embrace rather than betray our own values, our policy on Iraq would rest on a solid foundation, and a future Iraq could serve as a model for a regional political transformation. Otherwise, the Iraq file will continue to plague us.

American policy should not be oriented toward assuming control of Iraq, although if the INC and King Hussein are not resolutely supported we will eventually be forced to revert to war, to end Saddam's regime and occupy Baghdad. To avoid such an undesirable outcome, the United States must help Iraqis to create an army that will terminate the scourge of Saddam's regime. We should offer the Iraqi people the chance to determine their future, rather than condemning them to Saddam's oppression and to suffering the costs of his international aggression. Without such a plan, the United States will face a Hobson's choice: to accept any agreement contrived by international diplomats to preserve what remnants may remain of the controls on Iraq, or to go to war solo, to liberate and occupy an Arab capital. Neither option will further America's interests in the long run.

The Age of Modernity

Ultimately, U.S. policy in the Middle East is part of U.S. policy and purpose in the world. The collapse of the Soviet Union in 1991 indicted those around the globe whose politics were animated by common sources and alliances with communism. It was a historic opportunity for the United States to sweep away the two-hundred-year–old *Zeitgist* of the French Revolution and to assert in its place the superiority of the truly great revolution of the eighteenth century: the American. The world has been watching us for almost a decade, ready to be convinced.

Unfortunately, our Middle East policy has been diminishing our image in the world. One Egyptian newspaper boldly proclaimed in the summer of 1998 that it would be dangerous to side with the United States in the crisis with Saddam, because "by 2025 the European Union and China will have eclipsed the declining American-Canadian hemisphere."[4]

The United States has twice in this century vanquished the dark European politics from which pan-Arabic nationalism sprang. The defeat of communism was the second great blow; the first was the downfall of its Nazi model in World War II. These victories, complemented regionally by those of Israel, had so weakened pan-Arabic nationalism by 1991 that a vacuum was left in the Arab world, and the Middle East stood poised at an ideological crossroads. The United States had the opportunity to rid the Levant of this sort of politics. We had secured a victory for our values in the Middle East as an extension of our victory in the cold war.

The pan-Islamic fundamentalist revolutionaries, who embraced the totalitarian politics of the pan-Arabic nationalists but pursued different objectives, moved quickly to fill the void. But fundamentalism was weak. It came to power only in 1979, only in Iran, when America was in retreat. It can easily be defeated by a resolute Western challenge unabashedly asserting Western ideas.

Sadly, the United States defeats itself by proffering victories to both pan-Arabic nationalism and fundamentalism, and by embracing movements that advocate the ideas we discredited in the cold war. America has embarked on a policy of weakness in the Middle East; so afraid are we of the fundamentalist challenge that we have resigned ourselves to the immutability and resilience of pan-Arabic nationalist politics.

This resignation has led America to offer a paradoxical response to the Middle Eastern totalitarian challenge. We do not sweep aside those who most opposed liberal democracy in World War II and the cold war; we do not herald the antitotalitarian ideas that led us to victory; rather, we salvage the tyrants and peddle the politics of those whom we defeated. At the end of the cold war, the United States embarked on a policy of appeasing our defeated adversaries in the Middle East, wishfully to stem the surging fundamentalist tide. What has gone awry in Iraq policy is a consequence of this illogical strategy. The United States continues to view pan-Arabic nationalism as a force to domesticate and stabilize and to serve as a bulwark against other totalitarian movements.

By embracing the diminished politics and politicians that we defeated in the cold war, the liberal democracies of the West betray a sense of shame for our Western ideas. We confound our friends with our enemies, and we persuade many in the region that it is the kiss of death to be too closely allied with the United States. Opposing us, conversely, elicits respect from others and deference from ourselves. The Middle East is rapidly becoming a battlefield that disgraces and undermines our victory in the cold war.

Notes

CHAPTER 1: INTRODUCTION

1. Interview with Sandy Berger, *Face the Nation*, CBS News, November 16, 1997.

2. R. W. Apple, "Clinton Is Proud of Foreign Policy, Raising Eyebrows Everywhere," *New York Times*, December 18, 1997.

3. Berger, *Face the Nation*.

4. Carol Morella, "Iraq's Latest Adventure—A 'Marker' for the Arab World," *USA Today*, February 27, 1998.

5. *Town Hall Meeting*, CNN broadcast, February 18, 1998.

6. Jeffrey Smith, "Annan's Accord Is Spare on Details," *Washington Post*, February 25, 1998, p. A22.

7. Ibid.

8. John M. Gochko, "Annan Predicts Success; U.S. Says Questions Remain on Pact," *Washington Post*, February 24, 1998, p. A17.

9. John Lancaster, "Iraqis Happy with Pact on Inspections," *Washington Post*, February 24, 1998, p. A17.

10. "Reversing Course on Iraq," Editorial, *Washington Post*, February 26, 1998, p. A14.

11. Paul Johnson, *Modern Times: The World from the Twenties to the Nineties* (New York: HarperCollins, 1983).

12. The ferment produced by such an influx erupted in the rise of the Abbasid caliphate and gave birth to Shi'ite Islam, with its heavy emphasis on in-

terpretation and learning. Many great thinkers, new movements, and ideas emerged under the encouragement of the Abbasids and their successors.

13. See Denison B. Hull, *Digenis Akritas: The Two-Blood Border Guard* (Athens, Ohio: Ohio University Press, 1972). Perhaps the best example of the ferment triggered by this flow was the rich tradition of *Akritai* (border guard) ballads, laced with allusions to Christian factionalism (Manichean and Paulician struggles), cultural interaction, and ethnic mingling. The recurring name of the chief hero of these ballads was Digenis Akritas, literally, "biethnic border guard."

CHAPTER 2: THE SPENT STORM

1. President Bush said, "And there's another way for the bloodshed to stop, and that is for the Iraqi military and the *Iraqi people* to take matters into their own hands and force Saddam Hussein, the dictator, to step aside." [Emphasis is mine.] President George Bush, speech to the employees of the Raytheon Missile Systems plant in Andover, Massachusetts, February 15, 1991. The speech can be accessed on the internet at www.csdl.tamu.edu/bushlib/papers/1991/91021504.html.

2. Interview with Wafiq Samaraii, *Peter Jennings Reporting*: "Showdown with Saddam," ABC News, February 7, 1998. (Rebroadcast of original June 26, 1997, version entitled "Unfinished Business.")

3. Interview with Brent Scowcroft, *Peter Jennings Reporting*: "Showdown with Saddam," ABC News, February 7, 1998. (Rebroadcast of original June 26, 1997, version entitled "Unfinished Business.")

4. Randy Stearns, "The CIA's Secret War in Iraq," *ABC News Special Report*: "Showdown with Iraq, 1998"; available from http:/www.ABCNews.com.

5. See President Bush's opening statement at a White House news conference, Washington, D.C., April 16, 1991.

6. Iraqi National Congress information, August 1997. Also, author's interviews with Ahmad Chalabi, president of the INC, and Nabil Mussawi, director of INDICT, September 1, 1998. Both men said that these figures conservatively understated the reality.

7. Jim Hoagland, "How the CIA's War on Saddam Collapsed," *Washington Post*, June 26, 1997, p. A21.

8. So stunned were the Iranians at a request for cooperation from the United States that they refused, believing it a hoax of some sort. They demanded that they see a real American representative to prove that this request really came from the U.S. government. U.S. government representatives, however, are prohibited from meeting with Iranian government representatives. Thus, the INC brought the U.S. and Iranian representatives to the Khadra Hotel in Salaheddin and placed each at the opposite ends of a long corridor; the U.S. representative then placed the written request in the INC representative's hand, who carried it over to the Iranians, who only with such visible confirmation actually believed the message was genuine. See ibid.

9. Walter Goodman, "Iraqi Leader's Enemies: Far from a United Front," *New York Times*, June 26, 1997, p. B6.

10. Hoagland, "How the CIA's War Collapsed."

11. Interview with Ahmad Chalabi, *Peter Jennings Reporting*: "Showdown with Saddam," ABC News, February 7, 1998. (Rebroadcast of original June 26, 1997, version entitled "Unfinished Business.")

12. John Lancaster and David Ottaway, "With CIA's Help, Group in Jordan Targets Saddam," *Washington Post*, June 23, 1996, p. A1.

13. Robin Wright, "Jordan's King Aims to Organize Foes of Saddam Hussein," *Los Angeles Times*, December 7, 1995, p. A4.

14. Interview with Robert Pelletreau, *Peter Jennings Reporting*: "Showdown with Saddam," ABC News, February 7, 1998. (Rebroadcast of original June 26, 1997, version entitled "Unfinished Business.")

15. Senator Charles Robb, in Hearings on U.S. Policy toward Iraq, Subcommittee on the Near East and South Asia, Committee on Foreign Relations, U.S. Senate, March 2, 1998.

16. Interview with John Deutch, *"Peter Jennings Reporting*: "Showdown with Saddam," ABC News, February 7, 1998. (Rebroadcast of original June 26, 1997, version entitled "Unfinished Business.")

17. Interview with Massoud Barzani, *Peter Jennings Reporting*: "Showdown with Saddam," ABC News, February 7, 1998. (Rebroadcast of original June 26, 1997, version entitled "Unfinished Business.")

18. Samaraii, "Showdown with Saddam."

19. Scott MacLeod, "Gore to Rebels: We're with You, Maybe," *Time*, August 11, 1997.

20. Martin Indyk, address to the Soref Symposium, Washington Institute for Near East Policy, May 18, 1993.

21. Edward P. Djerejian, statement before the Subcommittee on Europe and the Middle East of the House Foreign Affairs Committee, March 9, 1993, in *U.S. Department of State Dispatch*, March 15, 1993.

22. Author's interviews with Warren Marik, March 7, 1998, and with Ahmad Chalabi, April 28, 1998.

23. Hoagland, "How the CIA's War Collapsed."

24. Author's interview with Warren Marik, March 7, 1998. See also Patrick Cockburn, "The CIA's Bungle in Baghdad," *The Independent*, April 11, 1997, p. 17.

25. Interview with General Adnan Nuri, *Peter Jennings Reporting*: "Showdown with Saddam," ABC News, February 7, 1998. (Rebroadcast of original June 26, 1997, version entitled "Unfinished Business.")

26. Hoagland, "How the CIA's War Collapsed."

27. Pelletreau, "Showdown with Saddam."

28. Marik, March 7, 1998.

29. Stearns, "CIA's Secret War in Iraq."

30. U.S. officials felt he was both unstable and loaded with luggage from a

"checkered" past. See Christopher Dickey, "Enemies Like These," *Newsweek*, October 2, 1995, pp. 49–50.

31. John Snyder, "Extending a Hand: Jordan Welcomes Iraqi Opposition," *Washington Jewish Week*, November 30, 1995.

32. Kamaran Karadaghi, "Can King Hussein Persuade the U.S. to Back Him over Iraq?" *al-Hayat*, September 28, 1995, as cited in *MidEast Mirror*, September 18, 1995, p. 16.

33. Author's interview with Ahmad Chalabi, June 10, 1998.

34. The first such visit known *publicly* was in late November 1995, as reported by a number of Arab papers (such as *al-Quds al-Arabi* and *al-Hayat*). My information comes from a translation and compilation of these articles in the *MidEast Mirror*. See "U.S. Encouraged by Progress in Reconciling Feuding Iraqi Kurds," *MidEast Mirror*, November 21, 1995, pp. 11–12.

35. "Iraq: Return of the Prodigal Son," *MidEast Mirror*, February 21, 1996, citing *al-Hayat*.

36. On December 14, 1995, Hussein Kamal unveiled his plan for toppling Saddam and creating what he called a High Council of Salvation of Iraq. He opposed Kurdish autonomy, thus bringing him into conflict with King Hussein's plans for a federal Iraq, and he favored pursuing a conspiracy against Saddam within the Iraqi military. The INC and its member groups rejected this plan. The plan is described in "Israeli Intelligence Gathering in Northern Iraq Said to Have Prompted Syrian Warning to Iraqi Dissidents," *MidEast Mirror*, December 14, 1995, p. 16.

37. Patrick Cockburn, "Saddam Overthrow Botched by CIA," *Independent*, April 11, 1997, p. 1.

38. Chalabi, June 10, 1998.

39. Lancaster and Ottaway, "With the CIA's Help."

40. "Proposed Camp for Iraqis in Jordan Would Become 'Base' for Toppling Saddam," *MidEast Mirror*, March 25, 1996, p. 11, citing reports from *Asharq al-Awsat*.

41. "Jordan Hesitant about Adopting Defecting Former Chief of Staff," *MidEast Mirror*, March 25, 1996, pp. 11–12, citing reports from *al-Quds al-Arabi* and *al-Hayat*.

42. Lancaster and Ottaway, "With the CIA's Help."

43. Ira Stoll, "Albright Asked to Help Group Plot Overthrow Saddam's Regime," *Forward*, March 19, 1996, p. A1.

44. Cockburn, "Botched by CIA." This story was also reported by ABC News in *Peter Jennings Reporting*: "Unfinished Business," June 26, 1997.

45. "Reports Proliferate of Iraqi Executions," *Washington Times*, August 14, 1996, p. A16.

46. Cockburn, "Botched by CIA."

47. Secretary of Defense William Perry, on *NewsHour with Jim Lehrer*, September 17, 1996, as cited from "Evolution of U.S. Policy on Iraq, the Iraqi Op-

position, and Northern Iraq," *Policy Watch*, no. 219, Washington Institute for Near East Policy, September 19, 1996.

48. Stoll, "Albright Asked to Help."

49. "CIA Chief Says Iraqi Leader in Stronger Position," *USA Today*, September 19, 1996.

50. See Herbert Kremp, "The United States Finds Using Its Authority No Longer Has Effect—Is Its Influence in the Middle East Slipping?" Hamburg's *Welt am Sonntag*, October 6, 1996, p. 33; and Robin Wright, "Allies Seen as Eroding Sanctions against Iraq," *Los Angeles Times*, June 6, 1997.

51. R. W. Apple, "Clinton Is Proud of Foreign Policy, Raising Eyebrows Everywhere," *New York Times*, December 18, 1997.

52. Wright, "Allies Seen as Eroding Sanctions." See also "Jordan: Chirac Reportedly Asks King to Reconcile with Iraq," *al-Ittihad*, October 29, 1996, p. 1.

53. James Anderson, "A Crumbling Credibility in Iraq Relations," *Washington Times*, August 24, 1998.

54. John Goshko, "Iraq Accused of Holding Back Data; Earlier Optimism Doused by Top UN Inspector," *Washington Post*, June 19, 1998, p. A27.

55. Madeleine K. Albright, Opening Remarks before the Senate Appropriations Committee, Subcommittee on Foreign Operations, June 16, 1998; text can be found at website http://secretary.state.gov/www/statements/1998/980616a.html.

56. William J. Clinton, Letter from the President to Congress: "Status of Efforts to Obtain Iraq's Compliance with UN Resolutions, June 24, 1998"; text can be found at website http:/www.state.gov/www/regions/nea/980624_pres_iraq.html.

57. Congressional Letter to the President of the United States, June 22, 1998, signed by Senators Trent Lott and Jesse Helms, as well as Representatives Newt Gingrich and Benjamin Gilman.

58. The exchange between the reporter and Rubin was as follows: *Question*: "Are you confirming the report in the *Post*. . . . " *Rubin*: "How many times did you hear me use the word *apparent*, Jim? . . . I said the word *apparent* six times for a reason, Jim. You can draw your own conclusion." See James Rubin, U.S. Department of State, Daily Press Briefing, June 23, 1998.

59. "Crisis in Iraq: Statements by U.S. Officials," U.S. Department of State, February 23, 1998; text can be found at website http://www.state.gov/www/regions/nea/usquotes.html.

60. Barton Gellman, "U.S. Tried to Halt Several Searches," *Washington Post*, August 27, 1998, p. A1.

61. Scott Ritter, "The Final Straw," *Wall Street Journal*, September 3, 1998.

62. James Bone, "America Blocks UN Searches for Iraqi Arms," *London Times*, August 10, 1998.

63. "The Clinton administration has intervened secretly for months, most recently last Friday [August 7, 1998], to dissuade United Nations weapons teams from mounting surprise inspections in Iraq because it wished to avoid a new cri-

sis with the Baghdad government, according to knowledgeable American and diplomatic accounts." Barton Gellman, "U.S. Sought to Prevent Iraqi Arms Inspections; Surprise Visits Canceled after Albright Argued That Timing Was Wrong," *Washington Post*, August 14, 1998, p. A1.

64. Gellman, "U.S. Tried to Halt Searches."

65. Jim Hoagland, "Ritter's Resignation," *Washington Post*, August 27, 1998, p. A21.

66. "The Clinton Administration has repeatedly intervened since last fall to delay or prevent intrusive weapons inspections in Iraq by United Nations teams. . . . U.S. efforts to influence weapons inspections . . . are more extensive than previously disclosed. . . . Its efforts have appeared to have shifted toward avoiding confrontation indefinitely." Gellman, "U.S. Tried to Halt Searches."

67. David Rogers, "Congress Is Asked to Give Broad New Authority for Covert Operations," *Wall Street Journal*, July 17, 1998, p. 1.

68. Daniel L. Byman and Kenneth M. Pollack, "Undermine: Supporting the Iraqi Opposition," *Iraq Strategy Review* (Washington, D.C.: Washington Institute for Near East Policy, 1998), pp. 59–88.

69. Ibid., pp. 59–61.

70. Rogers, "Congress Is Asked."

71. Ibid.

72. The *Washington Post* reported as follows: "The U.S. intelligence community was withholding logistical help and specific information from [Ritter's] inspectors. . . .Worse, the administration was actively pressuring two foreign governments to stop providing special intelligence UNSCOM needed on the Iraqi Special Security Organization and Special Republic Guard units that conceal and guard Saddam's clandestine biological and chemical arsenal. There may be some method in this seeming madness: These same elite units guard Saddam as well, and the Central Intelligence Agency has repeatedly sought to penetrate and use them to stage a coup. Intelligence from agents in Iraq might be compromised at the United Nations, or Ritter's relentless pursuit of Saddam's trusted guards might interfere with agency coup plotters, the CIA worried." Hoagland, "Ritter's Resignation."

73. "Chirac Asks King to Reconcile," *al-Ittihad.*

74. Washington Institute for Near East Policy Presidential Study Group, *Building Peace and Security* (Washington, D.C.: Washington Institute for Near East Policy, 1997), p. 18.

CHAPTER 3: AT WAR WITH THEMSELVES

1. Amatzia Baram, "Territorial Nationalism in the Middle East," *Middle Eastern Studies*, vol. 26 (4), October 1990, p. 445.

2. Lisa Anderson, "The State in the Middle East and North Africa," *Comparative Politics*, vol. 20 (1), October 1987, pp. 12–13.

3. Ibid., pp. 1–18. See also Baram, "Territorial Nationalism," pp. 425–48.

4. Anderson, "The State in the Middle East," p. 13.

5. Charles David Cremeans, *The Arabs and the World: Nasser's Arab Nationalist Policy* (New York: Council on Foreign Relations and Frederick A. Praeger, 1963), pp. 303, 304.

6. Ibid., p. 307.

7. Ibid., p. 321.

8. An example of this placating behavior is seen in the repeated British attempts to enlist the mufti of Jerusalem, Hajj Amin al-Husseini, as a representative of Palestinian Arabs in the 1920s and 1930s. All these attempts actually encouraged and strengthened the mufti in his conflict with Britain.

9. Elie Kedouri, *Democracy and Arab Political Culture* (Washington, D.C.: Washington Institute for Near East Policy, 1992), pp. 67–70.

10. Ibid., pp. 40–42.

11. Ibid.

12. Ibid.

13. Bassam Tibi, *Arab Nationalism: Between Islam and the Nation-State* (New York: St. Martin's Press, 1997), p. 116.

14. Ivan Turgenev, *Fathers and Sons* (New York: Penguin Books, 1972; originally published 1862), p. 94.

15. Ivan Turgenev, *Rudin*, in Franklin Reeve, ed., *Five Short Novels by Ivan Turgenev* (New York: Bantam, 1961), pp. 73–74. Translation quoted in this volume comes from Isaiah Berlin, *The Sense of Reality* (New York: Farrar, Straus and Giroux, 1997), p. 218.

16. Fyodor Dostoevsky, *The Devils* (New York: Penguin Books, 1971, originally published 1871), p. 248.

17. Ibid., pp. 125–26.

18. David Roberts, *The Ba'th and the Creation of Modern Syria* (London: Croom Helm, 1987), p. 63.

19. Ibid., p. 71.

20. Ibid., p. 74.

21. A full text of the communique can be found in Nikolaos Van Dam, *The Struggle for Power in Syria: Politics and Society under Assad and the Ba'th Party* (New York: I. B. Tauris Publishers, 1996), pp. 146–51.

22. Anis al-Sayigh, *al-Hashimiyyun wa al-Thawra al-'Arabiyya al-Kubra* [*The Hashemites and the Great Arab Revolution*], (Beirut: 1966), p. 277–78, in Tibi, *Arab Nationalism*, p. 116.

23. Tibi, *Arab Nationalism*, p. 118.

24. Ibid., p. 206.

25. Ibid., p. 207.

26. Ibid., p.121.

27. The mufti is the supreme Muslim religious authority of Jerusalem.

28. See M. P. Waters, *Mufti over the Middle East* (London, 1942); and Joseph B. Schechtmann, *The Mufti and the Fuhrer* (New York, 1965).

29. Maximilien Robespierre, "Terror Is Nothing Else Than Justice," in Brian MacArthur, ed., *Historic Speeches* (New York: Penguin Books, 1996), pp. 183–84.

30. Maximilien Robespierre, "Death Is the Beginning of Immortality," in MacArthur, *Historic Speeches*, p. 186.

31. Ibid., p. 189.

32. A similar dynamic appears in other Arab countries embracing pan-Arabist ideology, as minorities—mostly non-Sunni—tap pan-Arabism to legitimize their internal repression against the majority. One such case involving Ba'thism is the 'Alawite rule over the vastly Sunni majority in Syria.

33. This condition obtains not only among Arabs, but Russians, Somalis, or Yugoslavs as well.

34. Abbas Kelidar, "States without Foundations," *Journal of Contemporary History*, vol. 28 (1993), pp. 315, 333, and 335.

35. M. Zuheir Diab, *Syria and the Future of the Middle East Peace Process: A Report* (Washington, D.C.: United States Institute of Peace, December 7, 1993), p. 5.

36. The link between the internal and external is described as follows by a French diplomat: "Assad relies, both domestically and at the regional level, on complex strategies and tactics based on community, tribal, clan, and family ties where interpersonal obligations are paramount. Over the last thirty years, the building of those ties . . . has determined and set the pace both for domestic public life and for external policy. . . . As 'Alawi power has strengthened, expanded, and at the same time dispersed over the entirety of Syrian territory, the community's tribal distinctness, based on occupation of a particular terrain, has been blurred to the profit of segmentation by clans, even families, whose networks of solidarity and alliance extend beyond traditional internal and external limits of the community." See Alain Chouet, "'Alawi Tribal Space Tested by Power: Disintegration by Politics," *Monde Arabe: Maghreb-Machrek* (January–March 1995), pp. 93–119, cited in "Special Report: Power and 'Alawi Cohesiveness," *FBIS*, October 3, 1995, p. 1.

37. Similarly, such was the case when Serbian Communists tried to avoid accountability in Yugoslavia by fomenting unrest and inciting ethnic tension.

38. Jacob Burckhardt, *The Civilization of the Renaissance in Italy* (New York: Penguin Books, 1990), p. 74.

39. Not only was the United States never a colonial power in the Middle East (though it played a large role in dismantling the French and British colonial presence there), but many former colonized nations, including significantly the United States itself, have amicable relations with their former colonizers. Israel has good relations with Britain and even with Germany, despite the unprecedented experience of the Holocaust and the damage done to the Jewish world by Britain's colonial policies on Jewish immigration to Palestine. East and Central Europeans have good relations with Russians, despite their bitter experience in the cold war. India and many Latin American countries similarly are on good terms with Britain and Spain, respectively.

40. Washington Institute for Near East Policy Presidential Study Group, *Building Security and Peace in the Middle East* (Washington, D.C.: Washington Institute, 1997), p. 18.

CHAPTER 4: IRAN, SHI'ISM, AND THE REVOLUTION

1. Bassam Tibi, *Arab Nationalism: Between Islam and the Nation State* (New York: St. Martin's Press, 1997), p. 110.

2. Ibn-Sinna (Avicenna), al-Farabi, Ibn-Tufayl, and Ibn Rushd (Averroes) all understood the danger of man's treading into the realm of the divine, while recognizing the appropriate realm man can and should master: they believed man is responsible for understanding and mastering his immediate environment. This concept was extinguished in the twelfth century by Sunni orthodoxy under the works of al-Ghazali, a fatalist who insisted that the divine determined everything.

3. See, for example, Edward Shirley, *Know Thine Enemy* (New York: Farrar, Straus and Giroux, 1997).

4. Henry Fielding, *Tom Jones* (New York: Penguin Books, 1985), pp. 130–31.

5. Sir Edward Gibbon, *Decline and Fall of the Roman Empire*, Dero Saunders, ed. (New York: Penguin Books, 1985), p. 144.

6. Ibid., p. 85.

7. Ibid., pp. 292–93.

8. Japan in World War II was not a fascist state; it was a religious totalitarian state based on a controversial mikadoist offshoot of Shinto, called the Showa Restoration. See: Mark Peattie, *Ishiwara Kanji and Japan's Confrontation with the West* (Princeton: Princeton University Press, 1975), p. 231; see also: Stephen King-Hall, *Western Civilization and the Far East* (London: Methuen and Company, 1925).

9. This policy strategy dates back seventy years.

10. This policy is also leading to another Arab-Israeli war, through tolerance and support for the PLO.

11. Muhammad Makiyah's work is being continued by his son Kanan Makiyah, in the United States.

12. Fouad Ajami, *The Vanished Imam: Musa al-Sadr and the Shia of Lebanon* (Ithaca: Cornell University Press, 1986), p. 197.

13. Muhammad Jawad Maghniyya, *Khomeini wa al Dawla al Islamiyya*, as cited in Ajami, *The Vanished Imam*, p. 198.

14. The tenth day of Muharram, observed as the 'Ashura holiday, commemorates the martyrdom of Hussein, son of Ali and grandson of the prophet Muhammad. Hussein was defeated in battle at Karbala and murdered by Yazid, the second of the Umayyad dynasty, which ruled Islam from Damascus. Contemporary Shi'ite Muslims mark this sacred anniversary with reenactments, passion plays, and self-flagellations. See E. C. Hodgkin, *The Arabs* (London: Oxford University Press, 1966), pp. 33–35.

15. Yitzhak Nakash, *The Shi'is of Iraq* (Princeton: Princeton University Press, 1994).

16. Housing the shrine cities, Shi'ite schools receive remittances from many sources, especially Indian Shi'ite communities and "corpse traffic"—the lucrative business of selling burial plots in the holy cities to Shi'ites worldwide.

17. Nakash, *Shi'is of Iraq*, p. 16. See also Juan Cole, "'Indian Money' and the Shi'i Shrine Cities of Iraq, 1786–1850," *Middle Eastern Studies*, vol. 22 (1986), pp. 461–80.

18. Nakash, *Shi'is of Iraq*, p. 152. During the 'Ashura observances of 1921, for example, the Persian Shi'ites in Kadhimaym refused to conduct their processions under the observation of King Faisal I, insisting that only Iranian consulate officials could preside. In contrast, the Iraqi Shi'ites invited the king.

19. Ibid., p. 18.

CHAPTER 5: PAST AS PROLOGUE

1. *al-Quds al-Arabi*, August 29, 1995, as cited in *MidEast Mirror*, August 29, 1995, p. 12.

2. Translation of King Hussein's address to the Jordanian and Iraqi people on Baghdad Television, August 23, 1995, in *Foreign Broadcast Information Service (FBIS)*, August 23, 1995.

3. Ibid.

4. Ibid.

5. Ibid.

6. Ibid.

7. *King Hussein Discusses Iraq with Journalists*, Jordan Television Network, September 16, 1995, in *FBIS*, September 18, 1995, p. 53.

8. Bassam Tibi, *Arab Nationalism between Islam and the Nation-State* (New York: St. Martin's Press, 1997), p. 206.

9. *King Hussein Discusses Iraq*, Jordan Television Network.

10. Speech by King Hussein, addressing the Royal Institute of International Affairs, Chatham House, London, February 27, 1996.

11. Ibid.

12. Ibid.

13. Ibid.

14. Yitzhak Nakash, *The Shi'is of Iraq* (Princeton: Princeton University Press, 1994), p. 111.

15. Ibid.

16. Ibid., p. 113.

17. See Kamran Karadaghi, "Jordan versus Syria,," *al-Hayat*, February 5, 1996, as cited in *MidEast Mirror*, February 5, 1996, p. 17.

18. "Saddam Hussein Did Not Feel Hashemite Threat until Hussein Kamal's Defection," *al-Majalla*, January 7, 1996, in *FBIS*, April 2, 1996, p. 30.

CHAPTER 6: COMMON CAUSE

1. Stated by Arafat at a student rally at Gaza University on October 25, 1994, as cited in *MidEast Mirror*, October 25, 1994, p. 18.

2. Wafa Amir, "PLO, HAMAS Call Strike to Protest Treaty," Reuters Wire Service, October 26, 1994.

3. Broadcast on Jordanian State Television, as cited in *MidEast Mirror*, October 25, 1994, p. 17.

4. Middle East Media and Research Institute, "Arafat's Summer Camps: A Video," videotaped from a Palestinian television broadcast, July 15, 1998.

5. Speech delivered by Saddam Hussein on National Day, July 14, 1997, as translated and distributed by Laurie Mylroie, *Iraq News*, July 16, 1997.

6. *Jerusalem Post*, July 7, 1997, p. 1.

7. Jay Bushinsky, "Palestinian Authority Hiding Saddam's Arms Secrets," *Jerusalem Post*, November 6, 1997.

8. *Palestinian Media Review*, November 6, 1997.

9. For more information on Iraqi Hashemite intentions in Syria before1958, see Michael Eppel, "Nuri a-Said and 'Abd al-Ilah's Ambitions in Syria," in Asher Susser and Aryeh Shmuelevitz , eds., *The Hashemites in the Modern Arab World: Essays in Honour of the Late Professor Uriel Dann* (London: Frank Cass, 1995), pp. 152–64.

10. The Hashemites ruled from the 1920s until 1958, excepting the interruption of the 1941 coup. Al Gaylani's pro-Nazi dictatorship lasted only a few months.

11. "Now That Syrians Have Revived Their Dreams in Northern Jordan: U.S. Forces Train on Rescuing al-Mafraq from Possible Syrian Attack," *al-Bilad*, October 4, 1995, p. 5, in *Foreign Broadcast Information Service (FBIS)*, October 3, 1995, p. 58.

12. Talal Salman, "Hashemite Intrigue," *a-Safir*, August 11, 1995, as cited in *MidEast Mirror*, August 11, 1995, pp. 17–18. Other sources confirmed that Syria was very concerned over Jordan's "winning" Iraq. See Ibrahim Hamadi, "Syria," *al-Wasat*, September 1, 1995, as cited in *MidEast Mirror*, September 1, 1995, p. 16.

13. George Seeman, "Interview with Khaddam," *al-Wasat*, November 17, 1995, as cited in *Mideast Mirror*, November 17, 1995, pp. 8–9.

14. Nabil Sabbagh and Thana' al-Imam, "Interview with 'Abd al-Halim al-Khaddam," *Radio Monte Carlo*, November 20, 1995, in *FBIS*, November 22, 1995, p. 45.

15. Christopher Dickey, "Enemies Like These," *Newsweek*, October 2, 1995, pp. 49–50.

16. Salih Qallab, "Syria Moves to Take Charge of Iraqi Dossier," *Asharq al-Awsat*, September 4, 1995, p. 3, in *FBIS*, September 7, 1995, p. 66.

17. Andrew Tarnowski, "Syria Fears Encirclement by Pro-U.S. Governments," Reuters Newswire, September 11, 1995.

18. Ibid.

19. "Spooks' War against Syria's Allies in Lebanon Linked to Israel and Jordan's U-Turn on Iraq," *Asharq al-Awsat*, September 6, 1995, as cited in *MidEast Mirror*, September 6, 1995, p. 6.

20. Safa Ha'iri, "British, Not CIA, Linked to Kamil Defection," *al-Watan al-Arabi*, September 22, 1995, pp. 18–19, in *FBIS*, September 25, 1995, p. 45.

21. Ibid.

22. Ibid.

23. Fouad Hussein, cited in "Saudi Irony," *al-Quds al-Arabi*, August 29, 1995, as cited in *MidEast Mirror*, August 29, 1995, p. 15.

24. Salih Qallab, "Syria Moves to Take Charge of Iraqi Dossier," *Asharq al-Awsat*, September 4, 1995, p. 3, as cited in *FBIS*, September 7, 1995, p. 66.

25. *Al-Quds al-Arabi*, August 29, 1995, as cited in *MidEast Mirror*, August 29, 1995, p. 15.

26. Aqba Ali al-Saleh, "Syria Seeking Assurances on Its Regional Role and Iraq's Future," *Asharq al-Awsat*, September 27, 1995, p. 1, as cited in *MidEast Mirror*, September 27, 1995, p. 15.

27. Khairallah Khairallah's op-ed, in *al-Hayat*, October 5, 1995, as cited in *MidEast Mirror*, October 5, 1995, p. 12.

28. "Al Kabariti Rejects Syrian Accusations," *Shihan*, November 25, 1995, p. 5 in *FBIS*, November 27, 1995, p. 48.

29. "Jordan, Defending Its Involvement in Iraq, Reminds Syria of Its Much Bigger Role in Lebanon," *al-Hayat*, September 25, 1995, as cited in *MidEast Mirror*, September 25, 1995, p. 19.

30. "Interview with al-Kabariti," *al-Quds al-Arabi*, September 22, 1995, as cited in *MidEast Mirror*, September 22, 1995, p. 13.

31. *MidEast Mirror*, November 22, 1995, p. 18.

32. Ibid., p. 19.

33. Pinhas Inbari, "Syria Shifts Its Dangerous Displeasure to Jordan," *Jerusalem Post*, November 29, 1995, p. 5.

34. *Al-Quds al-Arabi*, as cited in *MidEast Mirror*, November 22, 1995, p. 19.

35. "Syria's Khaddam Declines to Invite al-Kabariti," *Al-Muharrir*, October 9, 1995, p. 7, in *FBIS*, October 10, 1995, p. 67.

36. Ali al-Saleh, "Syria Seeking Assurances."

37. *Asharq al-Awsat*, September 27, 1995, p. 1, as cited in *MidEast Mirror*, September 27, 1995, p. 15.

38. *Al-Hayat*, September 10, 1995, as cited in *MidEast Mirror*, September 11, 1995, p. 15.

39. Robert Pelletreau interview with Khalil Maalouf, *al-Hayat*, October 13, 1995, as cited in *MidEast Mirror*, October 13, 1995, p. 15.

40. This is seen, for example, in the speeches of the leading cleric of the Lebanese Shi'ites until 1967, Sheikh Muhammad Taqi Sadiq of Abadiyyah.

41. In Nabatiyeh, a major Shi'ite city in southern Lebanon, Israeli troops were welcomed during the invasion in 1982 with showers of flowers.

42. Hence, solutions to the Lebanese problem offered by the United States and Israel that extend, rather than undermine, Syria's role in Lebanon only solidify Iranian and Syrian control of this important community, instead of steering it back to the hopeful disposition it had before 1983–1984. This also highlights the degree to which Israel's 1996 Operation Grapes of Wrath was a deadly miscalculation: Israel should have attacked Syrian positions in such a way as to encourage those who sought to wrench themselves free of the Syrian and Iranian stranglehold. Instead, Israel granted Syrian forces immunity from attacks and focused on driving the Shi'ite communities of the south into a mass exodus, to Beirut. This move played directly into Syria and Iran's hand—driving the Shi'ites further into their control.

43. Speech delivered by King Hussein to members of the (unelected) lower house of the Jordanian parliament, as cited in *MidEast Mirror*, April 24, 1996.

44. "Iraq: Views on Hashemites, Future of Iraq," *al-Majallah*, January 7, 1996, pp. 28–29, as cited in *FBIS* April 2, 1996, p. 34.

45. Salwa al-Ustuwani, "A-Shar Informed Rafsanjani of Egypt's Support for Syrian-Iranian Coordination over Iraq," *Asharq al-Awsat*, September 10, 1995, p. 4, as cited in *FBIS*, September 12, 1995, p. 1.

46. Samir Ragab, *al-Gomhuriya*, August 28, 1995, as cited in *MidEast Mirror*, August 29, 1995, p. 16.

47. Makram Mohammad Ahmad, Editorial, in *al-Akhbar*, August 31, 1995, as cited in *MidEast Mirror*, August 31, 1995, p. 16.

48. Ibrahim Hamidi, *al-Wasat*, September 1, 1995, as cited in *MidEast Mirror*, September 1, 1995, p. 16.

49. Abderrahman al-Rashed, in *Asharq al-Awsat*, August 14, 1995, as cited in *MidEast Mirror*, August 14, 1995, p. 14.

50Ibid.

51. *Asharq al-Awsat*, August 14, 1995, as cited in *Mideast Mirror*, August 14, 1995, p. 12.

52. *al-Hayat*, January 16, 1996, as cited in *MidEast Mirror*, January 16, 1996, p. 16.

53. *Asharq al-Awsat*, February 5, 1996, as cited in *MidEast Mirror*, February 5, 1996, p. 14.

54. For example, Mubarak and Assad met immediately after the Jordanian-Israeli treaty was announced. During the press conference the two blasted King Hussein, calling him a heretic (*kufr*) for signing a separate peace with Israel. It was ironic that Egypt, which had signed a peace treaty alone with Israel fifteen years earlier, accused Jordan of making a separate peace. More ironic was to hear Assad, an 'Alawite, accusing a descendent of the Prophet Muhammad of being a heretic!

55. "King Hussein to Visit Saudi Arabia in Early December," *Jordan Times*, November 19, 1995, p. 1, in *FBIS*, November 20, 1995, p. 55.

56. *al-Majd*, January 29, 1996, as cited in *MidEast Mirror*, January 30, 1996, p.13.

57. *al-Quds al-Arabi*, February 14, 1996, as cited in *MidEast Mirror*, February 14, 1996, p. 12.

58. *al-Arab* and *al-Quds al-Arabi*, February 12, 1996, as cited in *MidEast Mirror*, February 12, 1996, p.16.

59. Saleh Qallab, "Reuniting the Ba'th," *Asharq al-Awsat*, September 4, 1995, as cited in *MidEast Mirror*, September 4, 1995, p. 14. Qallab even asserts that Assad is so intent on obstructing King Hussein that he would like to reunite the Arab Ba'th Socialist Party under the terms of the 1978 Pan-Arabic Charter.

60. David Gardner and Julian Ozanne, "Court of the Chameleon" (Interview with King Hussein), *London Financial Times*, October 17, 1995, p. 18.

61. Muhammed Sayyad, "Syria's Trump Card," *Akhbar al-Khaleej*, December 14, 1995, as cited in *MidEast Mirror*, December 14, 1995, p. 14.

62. *al-Majd*, January 29, 1996, as cited in *MidEast Mirror*, January 30, 1996, p. 13.

63. *al-Quds al-Arabi*, March 6, 1996, as cited in *MidEast Mirror*, March 6, 1996, p. 20. The reports were confirmed in *al-Hayat* the next day, as cited in *MidEast Mirror*, March 7, 1996, p. 11.

64. Walid Abu-Zahr, "al-Assad, Saddam Reportedly Meet on Border," *al-Watan al-Arabi*, May 3, 1996, pp. 30–31, as cited in *Mideast Mirror*, May 6, 1996, p.1.

CHAPTER 7: STRATEGIC CENTRALITY

1. Jay Bushinsky, "Arafat Said Trying to Forge New Eastern Front," *Jerusalem Post*, July 8, 1997, p. 1.

2. "The Palestinian Revolution arose to resurrection starting in 1974, and it draws its strength as the greatest revolution of the twentieth century from the Nicaraguan Revolution." Yassir Arafat, on website Israel on Line, as cited in *Mivzak*, June 8, 1997.

3. "Oh Allah, destroy America for she is ruled by Zionist Jews. . . . Allah shall take revenge on behalf of his prophet against the colonialist settlers who are the sons of monkeys and pigs." Ikrama Sabri, as broadcast on Palestinian Broadcasting Corporation, July 7, 1997.

4. Regarding the hunting down of Iraqi opposition figures, see Jay Bushinsky, "Iraqi Dissidents: U.S. Must Kill Saddam—An Interview with Nabil Mussawi," *Jerusalem Post*, November 17, 1997. Regarding the PLO's complicity in evading UNSCOM inspections, see Jay Bushinsky, "Palestinian Authority Hiding Saddam's Arms Secrets," *Jerusalem Post*, November 6, 1997.

5. Bushinsky, "Hiding Saddam's Arms Secrets."

6. Saddam's National Day Speech, July 14, 1997, as translated and distributed by Laurie Mylroie, in *Iraq Watch*.

7. See David Wurmser, *Coping with Crumbling States* (Washington, D.C.: Institute for Advanced Strategic and Political Studies, 1996).

8. Robert Pelletreau's interview with Khalil Maalouf, *al-Hayat*, October 13, 1995, as cited in *MidEast Mirror*, October 13, 1995, p. 16.

9. Kamran Karadaghi, "PKK Attacks on KDP in Northern Enclave," *al-Hayat*, August 29, 1995, as cited in *MidEast Mirror*, August 30, 1995, pp. 13–14.

10. "SAIRI Defends Badr Forces' Presence in North," *Voice of Rebellious Iraq*, November 15, 1995, in *Foreign Broadcast Information Service (FBIS)*, November 16, 1995, p. 24. A few days later, al-Hakim confirmed the forces' presence in northern Iraq; Salah Salamah, "Interview with Muhammad Baqr al-Hakim," *Paris Radio Monte Carlo*, October 23, 1995, in *FBIS*, October 25, pp. 35–36.

11. Ghassan Attiyah, "Iran Seen Affirming Pivotal Role," *al-Quds al-Arabi*, April 1, 1996, as cited in *MidEast Mirror*, April 1, 1996, p. 15.

12. *Peter Jennings Reporting*, ABC News, June 26, 1997.

13. Bushinsky, "Arafat Trying New Eastern Front."

14. Precisely such a strategy has been pursued against Israel by Syria, with some success, in Lebanon.

15. It was the PKK that triggered the fighting in the fall of 1995 that undermined the Dublin agreement and guaranteed the continuation of the inter-Kurdish feud.

CHAPTER 8: DEFEATING DESPOTISM

1. Edmund Burke, *Reflections on the Revolution in France* (New York: Penguin Books, 1968), pp. 106, 107, 115, 177, 120–21.

2. David M. Ransom, "Our Solution to the Saddam Stalemate," *Washington Post*, April 6, 1998, p. A25.

3. The "new Middle East" idea peddled by Shimon Peres is another iteration of this recurrent radical utopian theme.

4. Cairo Middle East News Agency, August 12, 1998, as cited in *Foreign Broadcast Information Service (FBIS)*, August 12, 1998.

Index

Newton, David, 38
Nicaragua, 63
Nuri, Adnan, 20, 21, 23, 130

Oil, 55, 56, 117, 126
Operation Provide Comfort, 11
Oslo peace process, 96, 97
Ottoman Empire, 49, 86, 93, 127.
    See also Great Arab Revolt

Palestine Liberation Organization
    (PLO): alliances with Iran, Iraq,
    and Syria, 98, 117–18; charac-
    teristics, 107; Christians and,
    107, 108; Hashemites and, 90,
    95; hiding of Iraqi documents,
    98; Hussein, Saddam and, 98,
    118; Iraqi Ba'thists and, 95; Is-
    rael and, 95, 96, 123–24; Jordan
    and, 90, 95, 96, 97, 123–24; in
    Lebanon, 109; muftis, 96–97;
    Shi'ites and, 107–9; Turkey and,
    123–24; U.S. view of, 46; veto
    power over peace process, 99.
    See also Arafat, Yassir
Palestinian Authority, 46, 98, 99,
    118
Palestinians, 96
Paine, Thomas, 56
Pan-Arabic nationalism: Britain
    and, 77; characteristics, 44–45,
    51–54, 56, 60, 71, 93; European
    politics and, 132, 138; failure
    and effects of, 55–57, 58, 82, 87;
    Great Arab Revolt and, 86;
    Hashemites in Iraq, 54; history
    and goals, 46–47, 53, 84, 86–87,
    133; Hussein, King of Jordan,
    83, 92–93; in Iraq, 42–43, 83;
    Islamic fundamentalism and, 70;
    minority repression of majorities,
    148*n*32; as political culture for
    Arabs, 44–46; religion and,
    66–67; resistance to Britain, 49;

revolution of 1958, 89; in Syria,
    49; terror in, 55, 56, 87; tradi-
    tional Arab society and, 49; view
    of Iraqi Shi'ites, 89; Western and
    U.S. interests, 46, 134, 136, 138.
    See also Ba'thism and Ba'thists
Pan-Islamic revolutionary move-
    ment, 86–87
Pelletreau, Robert, 16, 20–21, 27,
    106, 122
Perry, William, 28
Persian Empire, 6
Persian Gulf War (1991), 1, 13–14,
    71–72, 73
Petra Bank of Jordan, 90–91
Pickering, Thomas, 35
PKK (Partiya Karghrane Kurdistan,
    or Kurdish Workers' Party), 122,
    124, 155*n*15
PLO. *See* Palestine Liberation Orga-
    nization
Political issues: "age of modernity,"
    6; anti-Americanism, 61–62, 70,
    72–73, 118, 127, 132, 133–34;
    appeasement, 49, 97; Arab con-
    flicts, 127; "center of gravity,"
    119–20; centralization, 86, 93,
    132, 135–36; factionalism,
    87–88; Middle East political cul-
    ture and alignments, 44–45, 103,
    106, 117, 118–19, 125; political
    stability and instability, 41, 43,
    46, 60, 118–19, 130, 134; reli-
    gion, 68, 71; totalitarianism,
    86–87, 106, 127, 131, 132–33,
    135, 138; utopianism, 51, 87,
    132, 135. *See also* Hashemites;
    Pan-Arabic nationalism; Political
    power; Revolutions
Political power: arrogance and, 71;
    centralization and decentraliza-
    tion, 86, 93, 132, 135–36;
    radical change, 50, 119; revolu-
    tionary nationalism, 49; social

About the Author

David Wurmser is a research fellow and the director of the Middle East Studies Program at the American Enterprise Institute. He has formerly served as director of the Research in Strategy and Politics Program at the Institute for Advanced Strategic and Political Studies; director of institutional grants at the Washington Institute for Near East Policy; and project officer at the U.S. Institute for Peace.

He has published numerous pieces in the *Wall Street Journal*, *Washington Times*, *SAIS Review*, and *Middle East Quarterly*, as well as a monograph on the Israeli army entitled *Why Israel Wins Battles but Loses the Peace*. Mr. Wurmser received his B.A., M.A., and Ph.D. degrees all from Johns Hopkins University.

A Note on the Book

This book was edited by
Cheryl Weissman of the publications staff
of the American Enterprise Institute.
The index was prepared by Julia Petrakis.
The text was set in Bodoni.
Northeastern Graphic Services, Inc., set the type,
and Edwards Brothers, Incorporated,
printed and bound the book,
using permanent acid-free paper.

The AEI Press is the publisher for the American Enterprise Institute for Public Policy Research, 1150 Seventeenth Street, N.W., Washington, D.C. 20036; *Christopher DeMuth*, publisher; *Ann Petty*, editor; *Leigh Tripoli*, editor; *Cheryl Weissman*, editor; *Alice Anne English*, managing editor; *Susanna Huang*, editorial production assistant.